THE PREACHING TRADITION

A Brief History

DeWitte T. Holland

ABINGDON PREACHER'S LIBRARY

William D. Thompson, Editor

ABINGDON
Nashville

The Preaching Tradition: A Brief History

Copyright © 1980 by Abingdon

Library of Congress Cataloging in Publication Data

HOLLAND, DEWITTE TALMAGE, 1923–
  The preaching tradition.
  (Abingdon preacher's library series)
  Bibliography: p.
  Includes Index.
  1. Preaching—United States—History.
  2. Preaching—History. I. Title.
BV4208.U6H57   251'.00973   80-16339

ISBN 0-687-33875-1

Unless otherwise noted, scripture quotations are from the Revised Standard Version
of the Bible, copyrighted 1946, 1952, © 1971, 1973.

MANUFACTURED BY THE PARTHENON PRESS AT
NASHVILLE, TENNESSEE, UNITED STATES OF AMERICA

THE PREACHING TRADITION

Abingdon Preacher's Library

CONTENTS

EDITOR'S FOREWORD

Preaching has captured the attention of increasingly large segments of the American public. Lay parish committees seeking pastoral leadership consistently rank preaching as the most desirable pastoral skill. Seminary courses and clergy conferences on preaching attract participants in larger numbers than ever. Millions of viewers watch television preachers every week.

What is *good* preaching? is the question of both those who hear it and those who do it. Hearers answer that question instinctively, tuning in the preacher who meets their needs, whether in the pulpit of the neighborhood church or on a broadcast. Preachers need to answer more intentionally.

Time was that a good thick book on preaching would do it, or a miscellaneous smattering of thin ones. The time now seems ripe for a different kind of resource—a carefully conceived, tightly edited series of books whose scope covers the homiletical spectrum and whose individual volumes reveal the latest and best thinking about each specialty within the field of preaching. The volumes in the Abingdon Preacher's Library enable the preacher to understand preaching in its historical setting; to examine its biblical and theological underpinnings; to explore its spiritual, relational, and liturgical dimensions; and to develop insights into its craftsmanship. Designed primarily for use in the seminary classroom, this series will also serve the practicing preacher whose background in homiletics is spotty or out-of-date, or whose preaching needs strengthening in some specific area.

William D. Thompson
Eastern Baptist Theological Seminary
Philadelphia, Pennsylvania

I. INTRODUCTION

First of all it should be noted that the office of preaching is excellent, necessary, and agreeable to God, and that it is profitable to the preacher himself and useful to souls, and, lastly, that it is very difficult to reach perfection in preaching.
—Humbert de Romans

These pointed words about the office of preaching came from the master general of the Dominican Order of Preaching about A.D. 1250 and they preface his *Treatise on Preaching,* which, with minor revisions, could be used as a homiletics text today. Humbert knew whereof he spoke, for he had the responsibility of managing a large preaching order, assigning each friar to a preaching mission, and supervising the training of each member. His words might have been spoken by any or all of our present-day American seminary presidents, all of whom, it is likely, would wholeheartedly agree with Humbert that it is very difficult to reach perfection in preaching. They know well that preaching is the main area in which their graduates need additional help. They hear the continuing pleas from the churches, "Send us someone who can preach!"

The ability to communicate well and to preach effectively continues to head the list of the requisite qualities, as reported in survey after survey of churches seeking ministers. A church wants in its minister, of course, an able business administrator, a frequent and caring home visitor, a dynamic leader for the youth program, and an able scholar. But congregations are willing to make allowances in these areas to get good preaching; they will forgive much to have *exciting* preaching. They know that preaching in the context of liturgy is that point where all the training, all the thinking, and all the resources of mind, body, and spirit of the minister should come together to provide an opportunity for the experience of the living Word for the congregation.

Where the Word is preached, God is present to do his mighty works. Preaching serves to fulfill the church's responsibility for communication; its function is to explain the gospel to the church, to share it outside the church, and to make clear the teaching of Jesus.

The Scriptures are explicit on the basic content of preaching. They tell us what to say, but they do not mandate how it is to be said. The minister is free in any given case to provide the most effective means of communicating the gospel and to choose when, where, and how to preach. Quite clearly, the gospel message can be heard and appropriated in ways other than through a sermon preached to a group of people in a worship setting. This book is not concerned with those other ways. Our concern is with preaching in a worship context.

This work attempts to aid theological students and other persons interested in the church to obtain a historical perspective on preaching; to explore its strengths; to discover those things that sap its energies and to learn how to control them; to understand what it is and what it is not; to discern what it can do and what it should not be expected to do. This volume aims to help the student develop a global view of the office of preaching. With such a view, a person can relate preaching to other studies: biblical, theological, historical, ethical, linguistic, and the like.

Our plan is to trace American preaching from its ancient heritage to its present condition. Little space is given to the Eastern church after A.D. 1054 or to the European church in the post-Reformation period, since those activities have only indirectly affected the development of the American church and its preaching. The observations, descriptions, and interpretations recorded here come from the point of view of a university communication teacher with advanced training in rhetoric, a professional degree in theology from a neo-orthodox seminary program, twenty-five years of association with professional ecumenical groups, and three decades of itinerant ministry. Care has been taken in an attempt to be open and catholic in reporting all points of view fairly. Each heritage, however, is provincial from some point of view, and it is quite likely that some readers will see cultural, philosophical, and theological slanting in these pages.

Research for the book has involved the use of a great store of works—mostly secondary—on preaching: books, magazines, journals, newspapers, pamphlets, and recordings. Sources that are quoted directly and indirectly are cited in the notes. Using the suggested reading list, a student may go beyond the narrow limitations here to find extensive materials on people, churches, periods, or particular events in the history of preaching. Many persons and events have been omitted by choice; supporting detail on others could not be covered in the space allowed. Further, we have little or no information on many outstanding preachers whose records have been lost or destroyed in the turmoil of church history, particularly before the Renaissance. Moreover, while we do have material on most of the exceptionally great preachers and some on the near-greats, there is no information extant on 99 percent of the priests and ministers who, through the years, have preached faithfully and effectively without great public acclaim in country, village, and city. In the final accounting, those are the people who have been largely responsible for the preaching of the gospel and through whom God has worked his redemptive purposes.

The hope of this book is that the reader will discover these basic ideas about the nature and the practice of preaching.

1. Preaching is inherent in the nature of the church, and the church preaches in order to fulfill its mission.

2. The proclamation (the *kerygma*) and the teaching (sometimes called the *didache*), markedly different from each other, are both a part of the preaching function of the church; both are suitable, but under different conditions. The distinction is *content*—not mode of delivery, place, or time of communication.

3. Preaching is for people in a given circumstance, and that circumstance determines in some measure what they will comprehend and/or accept. One does not preach *in general*, but to people with unique needs, in particular settings.

4. Preaching works; when adjusted and brought home to the needs of people, it permits God to work in changing human behavior.

There is nothing wrong with preaching but poor preaching and the fact that churches permit poor preaching to continue.

5. Preaching, rightly done, fulfills and exhilarates not only the congregation but the preacher. Preaching, rightly done—though it may not reach the perfection spoken of by Humbert—opens the way for the redemptive presence of the living Word.

The heritage of Christian preaching begins quite early in the history of Judaism, and we must turn to that era to begin tracing its development to our present situation in twentieth-century America. In that tracing we may gain a perspective from which to proclaim to others what God himself has to say to them.

I. PREACHING: THE EARLY HERITAGE

PROPHETIC PREACHING

Preaching has not always been practiced the way it is today. Like every other phase of the church's life, it has undergone changes both profound and subtle. To be able to evaluate and to profit from them, it is important to know what the church was, how it got that way, and what difference those changes make. To describe these things is the task of this book. If we would understand preaching today, we must examine its heritage. Before the time of the Old Testament prophets, there were messengers of God who, by a free use of the term, might be called preachers. Enoch, the seventh from Adam, "prophesied"; Noah was called a "preacher of righteousness." Moses received a distinct commission when he was charged to take God's message to Pharaoh, and he became the guide of Israel not only with his rod but with his word. He spoke for God to the people, and for them to God. Aaron might be considered the prototype of the Israelite priesthood, and there is evidence that he and Moses were assisted by a body of prophet preachers. At this early date we can note evidences of two kinds of preaching ministry—prophetic and liturgical. Missionary/evangelical preaching was to come later.

Eventually the ark of the covenant fell into Philistine hands, the priesthood became corrupt, and then practically extinct. The Mosaic ritual, which had been divinely ordained for instruction, had been neglected and diverted to questionable use. The nation needed instruction in the true nature of religion. And so the prophets, from whom we really date our modern Christian preaching practices, began their task of teaching and exhorting.

We need to be aware that the prophets, like Moses, appeared with a distinct commission: They were to remind the people of their sins, exhort them to repent, and instruct them in religious, moral, social, and personal duties.[1] We tend nowadays, confusing our terminology, to identify prophecy with prediction. The words of the Old Testament prophets had, at times, predictive elements, of course, but these men were concerned primarily with "forth speaking," not with foretelling.

The great prophetic period in Israel's history began with Samuel (the last judge and the first prophet) about 1050 B.C. Then in the centuries that followed, such preachers as Samuel, Nathan, Elijah, Elisha, Joel, Micah, Isaiah, and Jeremiah warned, pleaded, rebuked, and encouraged their people, punctuating their messages with "Thus saith the Lord." They talked to the Hebrews through the days of Solomon's glory; through the division of the kingdom; through the bitterness that resulted from the division; through the Assyrian conquest, the Babylonian captivity, and the return to the promised land, always adapting their messages to the issues and context of the times.

The prophets of the captivity: Ezekiel and Daniel; and of the return: Haggai and Zachariah, had a double duty—to be watchers over the remnant of the Hebrews, keeping them steadfast as the world's religious hope, and at the same time, to represent this hope in some measure to the outside world. So they were in this sense missionary preachers, compelled to adapt the message of the chosen people beyond genetic and geographical boundaries.

Several things should be noted about the era of the prophet/preachers. It was with the rise of these men that preaching became an art for which training was provided in groups or schools. At Ramah, the home of Samuel; and at Gibeah; and later at Gilgal, Bethel, Jericho, and Mount Ephraim, companies of men gathered to study and to learn how to propagate the national religion. Apparently these schools of the prophets varied widely in enrollment, and the academics who attended seem to have belonged to no special class of people and to have represented no hereditary lines.

It bears mentioning that the prophets exercised a great amount of political influence and were a major corrective or check on the absolute power of the Hebrew kings. The prophets, or heralds of Yahweh, were independent of the kingship and were free to enter into open conflict with it. The priests were in a different situation; in fact, the chief priests, particularly in Jerusalem, were members of the royal administrative cabinet. As a result, they formed a support for the status quo and rarely were moving forces for social change or for the correction of social abuses.[2]

It is noteworthy also that during the period of the Exile, the synagogues arose and developed as substitutes for the Temple and, since there was a considerable need for instruction in the basics of the faith, scriptural exposition became a strong part of the liturgy. Earlier preaching had not made use of scripture as a basis for messages. There seemed to be little distinction between teaching and preaching, and out of this activity in the synagogue there arose a vast store of rich, expository literature, including the Targum and the Haggadah, still widely used materials in the Jewish faith.

The Jewish sermon as exposition of Scripture did not develop clearly until the postexilic period, but there seems to be a continuity of such usage into the Christian sermon. Only Judaism and Christendom make use of the freely spoken word as an essential portion of the liturgy, or holy acts of worship.

The synagogue setting in which sermons were presented was an oblong room, bare of images and paintings, with a desk on a low platform opposite the entrance. From this, scriptures were read and discourses delivered. Behind the platform stood the ark, or container of copies of the Law. The overriding mood of the building and the service was simplicity.

Until approximately 200 B.C., the scripture lesson was chosen from the Pentateuch; after that time the works of the prophets also were used. Sermons were delivered every sabbath and, on special occasions, on both Friday night and Saturday morning. Often younger rabbis led the activities of the assembly, and an elder sage would not appear until it was time for him to deliver the sermon.

By 100 B.C., sermons were well-established customs in Palestine and in the Diaspora. As the sacred language became unfamiliar and the history of their nation became remote to the Hebrew people, the sermon served as the chief means of instructing, guiding, strenghtening the faith, and refuting heretical views.[3]

The human bridge between the prophetic preaching of the Old Testament and the evangelistic preaching of Jesus was John the Baptist (4 B.C.?–? A.D. 30), whom Jesus called "more than a prophet." John was the son of a priest, but for some reason he spent his early years in the wilderness, living austerely, and it was there that he received the call from God which led him to undertake his prophetic preaching ministry.

> [He became] the centre of a religious awakening which deeply moved the region. An ascetic, he denounced the sins of those about him, spoke on imminent judgment with reward for the righteous and destruction for the wicked, urged repentance, and on the confession of their sins baptized the penitents in the Jordan. He gathered disciples about him, leading them in fasting and teaching them methods of prayer.[4]

And to him, beside the river, came Jesus seeking baptism.

JESUS' PREACHING

When Jesus went back to his hometown, Nazareth,

> he went to the synagogue, as his custom was, on the sabbath day. And he stood up to read; and there was given to him the book of the prophet Isaiah. He opened the book and found the place where it was written,
>   "The Spirit of the Lord is upon me,
>   because he has anointed me to preach good
>   news to the poor.
>   He has sent me to proclaim release to the captives
>   and recovering of sight to the blind,
>   to set at liberty those who are oppressed,
>   to proclaim the acceptable year of the Lord."
> And he closed the book, and gave it back to the attendant, and sat down; and the eyes of all in the synagogue were fixed on him. And he began to say to them, "Today this scripture has been fulfilled in your hearing."
> —Luke 4:16-21

Here is the link between the proclamation in the synagogue and the Christian sermon; the practice of Jesus is the primary connection between Old Testament prophecy and the preaching of the New Testament apostles. Human speech, as a means of divine teaching and proclamation, unites Judaism and Christianity, and Christian preaching centers in the example, teaching, and command of Jesus—"As you go, preach."

Following his baptism by John and the period of temptation and meditation in the wilderness, Jesus began his public ministry. It is quite clear in the synoptic Gospels that although he taught, healed, comforted, and fed, he was primarily a preacher—a man of words. He said to his friends, "Let us go into the next towns, that I may preach there also: for therefore came I forth" (Mark 1:38 KJV).

From biblical records, we can draw some important conclusions about Jesus' preaching. His central theme always concerned the kingdom of God, and he said that he came to illustrate, explain, simplify, clarify, objectify, and make plain for all to understand, the nature of that kingdom. There was a simple, natural quality about both the content and the language of his messages; he used familiar forms of address, abundant illustrations, questions and answers, and frequent metaphors and parables. He taught profound truths simply, but often poetically. We never tire of his story of the prodigal, and the image of the sower going forth to sow is made real for us every springtime. His preaching was direct, tactful, courteous, kind, and full of sympathy for humankind, yet in complete sympathy with God. He sought to bring heaven down to earth, that he might lift earth up to heaven. [5]

Our records are, of course, imperfect and incomplete, but they indicate quite clearly that crowds crushed to hear Jesus and listened to him with profound interest wherever he spoke—in the open air, from a boat, on a mountainside, by a well. He spoke to them with authority: "I say unto you," rather than "Thus said the Lord" or "It has been said to you of old." His preparation for his ministry, his conscious relationship to the Father, and his keen awareness of the source of his authority were all reflected in his confidence.

Prior to leaving his apostles for the last time, Jesus charged them to follow his example—to preach the gospel of the kingdom of God wherever they went in the world. At that time, Christianity was not established apart from Judaism, and Judaism was then one of the lesser of scores of mystery religions within the Roman Empire.

One of the most amazing and significant facts of history is that within five centuries of its birth Christianity won the professed allegiance of the overwhelming majority of the population of the Roman Empire and even the support of the Roman state. . . . [It] proved so far the victor [over Rome] that the Empire sought alliance with it and to be a Roman citizen became almost identical with being a Christian.[6]

APOSTOLIC PREACHING

Peter's address on the day of Pentecost was preaching in a new dimension. No longer was it necessary to say that the kingdom of God was at hand; the apostles now could proclaim that the kingdom had come; the promised Day of the Lord was ushered in. On that day the Christian church was born, and Jesus began keeping his promise to be with the disciples in Spirit and power wherever they communicated his word.

Jesus' choosing of the twelve apostles from among his many disciples was a notable circumstance; not only were these men to be with him physically in a special sense, but they were chosen to share his ministry as proclaimers of the kingdom of God. "You did not choose me," he told them, "but I chose you and appointed you" (John 15:16). The very use of the word apostle (one who is sent; a messenger) was significant. Pagan "philosophers" were preaching their doctrines, Jewish scriptures were replete with stories of "prophets," and the current Jewish religion had its "rabbis" and synagogue "preachers." But Jesus did not choose to use any of these titles that were associated with religious leadership. The term apostle was explicit and expressed very clearly that these were "sent men."

"Apostle" originally obtained only for the twelve; but later Paul, Barnabas, Andronicus, Junias, Silvanus, and Timothy were so called. Paul, particularly, sought to make it clear that his power and authority came from Christ himself—that he was an apostle by the will of God. His conviction of his personal call made him invincible. Later, such convictions sustained Luther, Francis of Assisi, Augustine, Savonarola, John Wesley, and thousands of other Christian men and women. It is a primary survival element of the Christian faith that its truth, its teaching, its message are in the care of witnesses who hold appointments from God; who are his messengers. Through such witnesses, both men and women, the gospel of God in Christ has persevered and prospered.

Unfortunately, we have almost no account of the actual preaching of the original twelve apostles. In the case of Peter there is some small record on which to make an analysis; on at least two occasions in Acts there is enough to suggest something of his style. His preaching appears to have been forthright and urgent, using a characteristic Hebrew style with vigorous verbs, concrete illustrations, and a minimum of abstractions.

As for Paul's preaching, we have a wealth of material for study. We have, at least in outline form, his speeches to the elders at Ephesus, before the Jews in Jerusalem, before the council, before Felix, before Herod Agrippa, and finally at Rome. Also, we are able to read his Epistles, which were essentially written sermons meant to be read in the churches to which they were addressed. Paul was first of all a preacher, as was Jesus; he gave preaching the primary place in his ministry. Immediately following his conversion he went to the synagogue and proclaimed Jesus the Son of God, and he continued preaching until the end of his life in Rome.

We learn from biblical records that Paul often used the style of an orator, moving his audience along so gently that his close reasoning was not obtrusive. He was quick to illustrate from materials close at hand—nature, poetry, art, war, athletics—adapting to the interests of the people he addressed. His words and figures suggest a cultivated man with careful rhetorical training. His unique background—Hebrew by birth, Roman by citizenship, and Greek in culture—eminently qualified him to carry the Christian gospel, developed in Hebrew form, into the Western world through Greek thought-patterns. The Christian gospel probably was just as much out of touch with the thought of the Hellenistic world then, as it often seems to be now, with our world. But Paul and others like him succeeded in interpreting Christianity to the contemporary Greek mind in terms that made its essential relevance and truth clear and desirable.

During the early part of the apostolic period, first in Jerusalem and later in Samaria, Damascus, and other cities as the disciples dispersed, much preaching took place in private homes, borrowed synagogues, rented buildings, and the like. Little is reported about discourses delivered or sermons preached; rather we read that the apostles simply told the story or spoke to people. Such apostolic preaching must have been as personal and direct as private conversation. While the content of the gospel message was clearly delineated, its manner of presentation was not. Presentation was and is a matter of discipline, not doctrine, and requires adjustments for effectiveness in varying situations.

The substance of New Testament preaching seems of particular importance to our study. Preaching near to Jesus in time and place is especially noteworthy to us. Was there a central theme, a uniform affirmation, a topic sentence of New Testament preaching, and if so, what is the warrant of that core? The benchmark work of C. H. Dodd, issued in 1936, sifted out the central ideas of all the Christian sermons recorded in the New Testament. Though the sermons were in thumbnail-sketch form, analysis revealed an essential unity in basic content, identified as the *kerygma*.[7] It is said that Dodd's approach marked the first known time that a single biblical concept had been related to all New Testament material.

The kerygma delineated by Dodd pointed to an irreducible core of New Testament preaching; the total New Testament is but its elaboration and clarification. There seems to be some variation among scholarly interpretations, but basically the kerygma involves these points.

1. The age of fulfillment, or the coming of the kingdom of God, is at hand.

2. This coming has taken place through the ministry, death, and resurrection of Jesus.

3. By virtue of the resurrection, Jesus is exalted at the right hand of God as the messianic head of the new Israel.

4. The Holy Spirit in the church is the sign of Christ's present power and glory.

5. The messianic age will shortly reach its consummation in the Second Coming of Christ.

6. Forgiveness, the Holy Spirit, and salvation come with repentance.[8]

This kerygma, or content, of preaching, may be neither ignored or diminished without destroying the Christian message. It is the standard by which the preaching of the church in all ages is to be measured; and when all or part of the standard is obscured, the church loses its voice of authority. This is the outreach message always to be used in the context of winning unbelievers. It was "by the foolishness of preaching [the kerygma]" or by the substance of the gospel, that God chose to save the believer.

Obviously the New Testament contains records of speaking, described as preaching, other than the kerygmatic variety. Apostolic preachers dealt, as do preachers today, with matters that pressed for attention, and they sought to apply the gospel to them. Paul did not preach to the Corinthian church about the falling away in Rome, nor to the Romans about corruption and factions in Corinth. Then as now, preachers dealt with inspiring the believers, building the church, applying the gospel in moral situations, and correcting misunderstandings, in addition to presenting the kerygma.

PATRISTIC PREACHING

With the passing of the apostles came the period we have come to call patristic—the era of the Church Fathers. The Fathers have been variously defined, but were usually prominent bishops and other Christians who formulated doctrines and codified religious observances. Their work is noted mainly for sound judgment, intellectual enthusiasm, and a sense of balance; in fact, during the Reformation, both Catholics and Protestants used their writings as a "court of appeals."

The entire story of the spread of Christianity in its first five centuries cannot be told; we simply do not possess enough information to report it. We think of it as a time of solidifying the gains made during the apostolic period beyond the confines of Palestine—notably in Antioch, Ephesus, Corinth, Alexandria, Hippo, and Rome. By the end of the first century A.D., Christians had spread throughout Asia Minor, and by A.D. 150, the Roman Empire was dotted with their churches. We know that when they became numerous enough to disturb political authorities of the empire, they suffered terrible persecutions and that the persecution under Diocletian, which began in 303, was the last and most severe. During the times of persecution holy records of the early years were burned or otherwise destroyed by both the Christians and their persecutors.

Our information is sketchy about Christian ceremonies, methods, and ideas for much of the first two hundred years. It was during the last half of the second century and the first part of the third, we believe, that significant changes in the form and context of Christian preaching came about. Church buildings were constructed and a set form and order of worship developed. Over the next few centuries outstanding preachers arose.

Justin Martyr (circa 100–165) was one of the first and perhaps the greatest of the Apologists. A teacher of Platonic doctrines and a student of philosophy, he opened the first Christian school at Rome. He defended the life of the church against its persecutors and its faith against rival beliefs.

Clement of Alexandria (150?–?220) was born a pagan, but represents for us a mystical and cultured Greek Christianity. He opened a catechetical school in Alexandria for the purpose of instructing candidates for church membership in the principles of the Christian faith. One of the earliest existing sermons is his homily on the wealthy, based on Mark 10:17-31.

Tertullian (160?–?230), an austere lawyer from Carthage, was converted at age thirty and thereafter devoted himself to a mastery of the Scriptures and Christian literature. He is credited with formulating Latin Christian thought and wrote a defense of Christianity, *Apologeticus*, inspired by Roman persecutions.

Origen (185?–?254) was born of Christian parents. When he was seventeen, his father was martyred. To prevent the youthful avenger from rushing out to meet the same fate, his mother hid all his clothes for a period of time, thus forcing him to remain in safe quarters. Probably as a result of this parental intervention he survived and later succeeded Clement as head of the Alexandrian catechetical school. He is reported to have been a superb teacher. He wrote prodigiously and is known as an allegorist, biblical critic, mystic, and Apologist.

Cyprian (200?–?258) is noted for his preaching works that dealt with practical problems of conduct and order. He was martyred in 258, ending his tenure as Bishop of Carthage.

Cappodocian Gregory of Nazianzus (329?–?389), son of a bishop, became a preacher in Constantinople when he was almost fifty years old. He was profoundly impressed with Origen's work and became famous in the East as a theologian. In fact, he was surnamed Theologus—the theologian.

Another Cappodician, Basil the Great (d. 379), friend of Gregory of Nazianzus and also well known in the East, is now recognized as the founder of monastic institutions.

Ambrose (340–397) was celebrated in the West, and his works included homiletical commentaries and hymns. He baptized Augustine on April 25, 387.

But there were two men who represent the pinnacle of patristic preaching—Augustine in the West and Chrysostom in the East. Augustine, who became Bishop of Hippo, did not begin to preach until he was thirty-six years old. In him, the Latin sermon matured and began to be developed as a unique form, akin to, but different from, the rhetorical tradition out of which he came. There exist some four hundred of his sermons (he often preached several times a day) as well as numbers of his commentaries, which were first delivered as homiletic addresses. His work *De Doctrine Christianus* was the first significant work on homiletics that delineated differences and similarities in rhetoric and preaching. His homiletical handbook, the fourth book of *De Doctrine Christianus*, endeavored to demonstrate that the sermon should be, first of all, an exposition of Scripture. He saw in the biblical authors a pattern of eloquence for the church and suggested that the Bible is largely a kind of sacred rhetoric, with its own ornaments, metaphors, and figures, which the preacher must learn to use. While trying to free preaching from rhetoric, he at the same time introduced into the homiletical tradition certain of the rhetorical categories, which continue to be a part of homiletics even now.

John Chrysostom of Antioch marks the summit of sacred eloquence in the Greek church of the patristic period; in fact, a good case could be made that he has not yet been excelled in the Greek church. Like Gregory of Nazianzus and Augustine, he was not a young man when he began his preaching ministry; he was trained as a rhetorician and became a preacher almost against his will. The church became convinced that God was calling him and insisted that he answer. His oratorical skills earned him the name Chrysostom (literally golden-mouthed), from the Greek *chrysostomos*. He was basically a Bible expositor, and a number of his discourses have been worked together into continuing commentaries on the Scriptures. His preaching was not confined to the sabbath. During festivals and on special days he delivered sermons every day of the week and his homilies on the book of Genesis are known to have been preached as a series, day after day. At that time, it was not uncommon to have two or even three sermons delivered before the same assembly, first by the presbyters and then by the bishop. Also, the people often were assembled several times on the same day to hear the Word expounded—morning, afternoon, and evening.

It is necessary to generalize about the preaching in a period when the practices were obviously quite diverse. On the whole, it was a time of preaching excellence—a time of rich and rapid growth in homiletical theory and skills and in the expansion of the church. As early as A.D. 150, Justin Martyr mentions preaching as a part of the regular liturgical services. Tertullian provides a reference to a sermon (discourse) of the martyred Bishop of Smyrna, Polycarp (69?–?155), who had been instructed by the apostles and actually had talked with many who had seen Christ. Eusebius, in the fourth century, collected the sermons of Irenaeus, who died in A.D. 202.

If we were to read the writings of the Fathers, sermons included, with the expectation of profound reasoning and clear analyses, we would be disappointed. Today, we would question their biblical understanding and interpretation. But Christianity was yet in its infancy, and each person is, to a certain extent, a product of the time in which he or she lives. The patristic sermons and writings (which were often oral discourses taken down stenographically) do have intrinsic worth, however, for they are rich in thought, energetic, elegant, and some are even examples of sublime oratory. They also cast light upon the history of doctrine.

The sermon came to have a traditional place in the church service, immediately following the reading of the psalms and lessons from the Scriptures. It was introduced by a short prayer for divine aid, as suggested by Augustine when he instructed the preacher to pray both for himself and for others, before beginning to teach.

> To this end before he loose his tongue to speak, he should lift up his thirsting soul to God that he may be able to discharge what he has imbibed and pour forth to others that wherewith he has filled himself.[9]

Apparently it also was customary, before the first sentence of the sermon, for the preacher to salute his people with "Peace be unto you," and for them to respond, "And with your spirit." Records show, too, that sometimes the sermon was preceded by a short benediction as in Chrysostom's fourth sermon to the people of Antioch, which began, "Blessed be God who has comforted your sorrowful souls." Quite often the preacher concluded with the doxology to the Holy Trinity.

As the sermon grew in importance, the portion of time it occupied was extended. Extant sermons, if we have them fully reported, generally would have required fifteen to twenty minutes for delivery; some possibly required an hour, but probably the average time involved did not reach thirty minutes.

Usually the message was based on the *scripture* that was read on the occasion; in rare cases the preacher took no text; and records show that sometimes several passages from the psalms, Epistles, and Gospels were brought together as the basis for the sermon. Generally, the expository method of preaching was used, with the preacher delivering a running commentary upon his text. In the expository sermons it was common first to develop the meaning of a given passage and then to follow through with an appropriate lesson or application for the particular situation or occasion. In some cases, the moral lesson was held until the conclusion of the sermon and introduced there through illustration and application, with great effect. In the homilies of Chrysostom and Augustine there are series of sermons, or connected discourses, upon whole books of the Bible, such as Genesis or one of the Gospels.

In addition to Scripture, *tradition* also came to be acknowledged as a basis for authority in preaching during the time of the Fathers. Tertullian, in his *De Corona Militis* averred, "If no scripture hath confirmed this, assuredly custom hath confirmed it which doubtless hath been derived from tradition."[10] Tertullian also spoke of observances that had no scriptural foundation and that he defended on the ground of tradition alone.

Generally the discourses of the Fathers were free and familiar, or direct. The Greeks called them "homilies," from a Greek word meaning "to converse in company." It was common for the people, when pleased by the words of a preacher, to applaud or to acclaim him vocally. Handkerchiefs were waved and garments were tossed in the air. (Surely some of our contemporay rock concert behavior is not derived from this practice!) Sometimes hearers responded to the messages with sobs, tears, and groans. Such a value was placed on the sermons of the more eloquent preachers that stenographers were employed to report their words, and copies were circulated and held for reading to other assemblies. No doubt some of the homilies of the Fathers have come to us through this manner.

Oddly enough, to the twentieth-century mind, it was usual for the preacher to sit and for the people to stand during the sermon. This practice varied in some churches, where both preacher and congregation sat. Most commonly, the speaker addressed the people from a sitting position in the ambo (one of the two pulpits on raised stands in the early church) or from the reading desk or episcopal seat. This was probably in imitation of the form of worship in the synagogue, where the teacher sat in Moses' seat, and of Jesus' habit of sitting down to address the multitudes, as suggested in several scriptural passages in the synoptic Gospels.

At first there were no schools for the training of the clergy; later, for a time, the only one was in Alexandria. By the end of the fourth century the Christian school in Antioch was formed and became a general center for professional Christian study. Eventually nearly all the leading preachers of the period pursued a long course of theological studies after having completed work at one of the great secular schools in Antioch, Constantinople, Athens, Rome, or even in one of the lesser cities. Especially notable in the curriculum of the great universities were the ancient languages and the rhetorical arts. Many of the Fathers were exceptionally well trained in rhetoric and oratory. Indeed, several had been teachers of the art—notably Augustine and Chrysostom. Rhetorical styles of the day were considerably more florid than agree with our taste and were not particularly suited to the simplicity of the gospel message. Secular rhetorical training, however, sometimes was carried over into the pulpit and some preachers were inclined to the overuse of fine language and figures of speech as ends in themselves, rather than as means of comunicating the Word. Nevertheless, Fenelon, the great French preacher of the seventeenth century, observed that, second to the Scriptures, knowledge of the Fathers would most help a preacher compose good sermons.[11]

After the times of Chrysostom and Augustine, Christian preaching ceased to show any remarkable power. Homiletical practices had been developed and reduced generally to theory. Preaching seemed to have gotten itself together and was able to stand on its own feet as a separate discipline. Nevertheless, it waned radically in the fifth century, with at least four factors contributing to that decline: (1) asceticism; (2) liturgy; (3) the emergence of Christianity as the state religion; and (4) the growth of the secular power of the church.

Christianity contains some inherent ascetic dimensions: Christians are urged to be in the world, but not of it. Meditation; contemplation; and prayer for an hour, for a night, or even for forty days were very real practices in the life of Jesus. After his conversion, Paul apparently went through a preparation period which included an extended period of contemplation, before entering his public ministry. Jesus, Paul, and the apostles practiced the contemplative life, but always as a respite from extended labors or as preparation for other work. Christianity is basically a going, doing, active, empirical religion with clear ethical imperatives; asceticism and contemplation are only parts of the Christian life.

Twentieth-century Trappist monk Thomas Merton, himself a Christian activist despite his monastic vocation, has given us a statement that describes the appeal of the contemplative life.

There can be no doubt that the monastic vocation is one of the most beautiful in the Church of God. The "contemplative life," as the life of the monastic orders is usually called today, is a life entirely devoted to the mystery of Christ, to living the life of God Who gives Himself to us in Christ. It is a life totally abandoned to the Holy Spirit, a life of humility, obedience, solitude, silence, prayer, in which we renounce our own desires and our own ways in order to live in the liberty of the sons of God, guided by the Holy Spirit speaking through our Superiors, our Rule, and in the inspirations of His grace within our hearts. It is a life of total self-oblation to God, in union with Jesus who was crucified for us and rose from the dead and lives in us by His Holy Spirit.[12]

In the early patristic period, however, young men feeling the call of God to Christian service often were drawn into a misguided monastic life of no service beyond the confines of the cloister. They were simply hermits, not differing greatly from those of ancient Egypt. Later they developed hermit cells with a communal center for worship. As a consequence of their withdrawal the church was denied the talents of hundreds of highly motivated young men who felt an inner urging to serve God through the church and were diverted into an inwardly turned monastic life. This powerful but mistaken impulse sent into the deserts and caves, and later into monasteries, thousands of earnest men, whose lives thereafter did not count in proclamation or in sharing activity, but were spent in penances and self-torture.[13]

Ceremonialism was the second factor affecting the decline of preaching. Unquestionably, liturgy communicates, but it communicates only with the initiated—those who understand the imagery and allusions of the ceremony. And while it may be an excellent means for assisting in public worship or for deepening emotional commitment to a basic value or idea that already has been created within a given hearer or audience, it is not designed to be persuasive to the uninitiated. Liturgical experience, no matter how moving, seldom creates new members of the community; it is communion for those already in union. It inspires people to practice the virtues symbolized in the ceremony only if those virtues already exist among the members of the liturgical group.[14]

As the preaching office began to be taken away from the majority of the clergy, primarily because of their poor background in skills needed for sermonizing, it fell to the bishops to do the preaching. However, since the bishops could not preach in all the churches with reasonable regularity, the parish clergy had to do what they were trained to do—preside over the liturgy. Thus as liturgy increased in usage, preaching as a separate proclamation of the kerygma diminished. The problem was not that the power of preaching had failed; it was that the clergy were not equipped to exercise that power.

When Christianity became the state religion, the church ceased to be a voluntary society and became coextensive with the civil community. Emperior Constantine I (280?–337), for a mixture of personal and political reasons, decided to follow the old political maxim, "If you can't beat 'em, join 'em." His policy of persecution had failed, and so, after a concerted effort to destroy the Christian movement, he recognized it, and in 313 made Christianity the official religion of the Roman Empire (not the *only* religion; that came later under other emperors). "From him the Church acquired the disposition to be authoritative and unquestioned, to develop a centralized organization and run parallel to the empire."[15]

The individual Christian could now profess the faith openly and meet freely with other Christians to worship. The church was now exempted from paying certain taxes, ecclesiastical courts were recognized (they also served as the United Fund of the day), and the treasures of pagan temples were given for Christian use. But imperial patronage and favor proved to be of dubious value. The changes made greater difference in the character of the church than in the character of the world. The church no longer could pretend to be a fellowship of the redeemed—a group markedly different in character from the larger society around it.

It was impossible for the church to assimilate all the Roman citizens who desired to follow their emperor in embracing his new faith. (Constantine had his children instructed in Christianity, but he himself was not baptized until he was on his deathbed). Thus, with large numbers of unregenerate citizens on the church membership lists, heavy emphasis began to be placed upon following the rites and regulations of the church, rather than on personal repentance and submission to the will of God. In that situation, the proclamation of the kerygma declined as membership in the church became identified as membership in the kingdom of God.

The fourth factor contributing to the decline of preaching was the growth of the secular power of the church after it became the state religion. In such position, it established and administered ecclesiastical courts, levied and collected taxes, planned and executed vast charities, and exercised considerable political power. Heresies had to be smoked out and offenders properly punished. All these functions required considerable manpower and executive clout since all citizens of the empire (except Jews) fell under the discipline of the church. Being so occupied, the church had little time, need, or disposition to preach.

These four factors contributing to the decline of preaching ushered in a millennium when, with rare exceptions, the pulpit was barren of great preaching personalities. These contributing factors continued to militate against preaching until the revival of the proclamation of the Word in the pre-Reformation and Reformation periods. Indeed, under conditions similar to those of the late patristic period, these elements still may work to the detriment of effective preaching.

II. PREACHING: DECLINE AND RENEWAL

THE DARK YEARS

The fall of Rome in A.D. 476 marked the end of classical civilization and the settling in of a period in the West called, for several reasons, the Dark Ages. Drastic political and social changes occurred, resulting in profound alterations in the lives of the people. Cities and towns suffered losses of population and wealth; agriculture became the main productive occupation; feudalism began to emerge; travel became extremely hazardous; war, arson, and plundering became common practices; famines were frequent, and plagues destroyed people and livestock; education and the arts suffered tragically. The nomadic German invaders, vigorous though they were, differed greatly from the cultivated people of southern Europe, and they succeeded in destroying most of the cities Rome had built in western Europe. In their place, many small kingdoms were established, most of which were short-lived.

> Life in this colorful, contradictory period was often like a pageant, a parade, or a long trip. People feared the dark; they believed in witches; they thought less of life on earth than they did of life in heaven. [They were] often childlike, often unfortunate; generally poor.[1]

For the reasons we have noted, by this time the prominence of preaching was already diminishing, and the sermon was being replaced by more formal liturgies and an increasing emphasis on the mass. The kerygma, or basic proclamation of the gospel, was largely ignored as sermons/homilies focused on the importance of churchly duties, special observances, relics, and the like. Christianity ceased to be basically an enthusiastic lay movement and became more and more an ecclesiastical institution. No immediate successors to the great preachers of the patristic period emerged, and during the early dark years preaching reached the lowest point in its history.

This is not to say that one skips from Chrysostom and Augustine to the end of Middle Ages to examine the history of preaching, however. One of the bright points of the time was the work of the missionary preachers who ventured beyond established diocesan borders and preached primarily to the unchurched, often at great personal risk. Columba (521–597), born in Ireland and trained in the Irish monasteries of Moville and Leinster, established a monastery in 563 on the Isle of Iona. From that base Christianity entered Scotland.

Earlier, Patrick (389?–?461) heeded a call (which came to him in a dream) to preach to the Irish. He trained in France and in 432 was sent by Pope Celestine I to serve as a missionary to Ireland. He founded churches and planted the faith throughout Ireland, introducing Latin as the language of the church there. A high level of Christian culture grew up in the Irish monasteries between the fifth and eighth centuries. Columban (540–615), an Irishman, at the age of only fifteen, took twelve companions into the Frankish area as missionaries and preachers.

Missionaries did not come to England until 597. In that year, Augustine (566-607), a Roman monk and a former slave, was sent by Pope Gregory I as a missionary to the English. He was especially effective in evangelical and missionary preaching and in establishing the policy of the Roman church in England. He founded the church at Canterbury and became its first archbishop in 601.

An Englishman, Benedictine missionary, and ecclesiastical statesman, Boniface (675–754) became particularly effective as a missionary preacher to Germany. He was called the Apostle of Germany, and rose to the rank of Archbishop of Mainz. He later resigned his position to rededicate himself to missionary preaching activity and was slain on a journey to the Netherlands by the people he sought to help.

Later, Anschar (801–865), trained in a monastery at Corbie in France, became an effective missionary preacher to Denmark, Sweden, and Germany.[2]

But despite the activities of the missionary preachers, church conditions on the home front were generally dismal. In many areas sermons were essentially abandoned and replaced by postils—very brief addresses delivered at the conclusion of the mass—something of a postscript to the total worship service.

When Charlemagne (742–814), king of Franks, conquered the German tribes between the Rhine and Vistula rivers and required them to accept Christianity, seeking to establish a Holy Roman Empire, he chose preaching as a primary tool for reform and for the restoration of health to society. He charged Alcuin (735–804), one of his ministers—a churchman and English scholar—to set up training for preachers, with the intent of reestablishing preaching as a viable force in society. In this task Alcuin drew very heavily from classical rhetorical theory and from Augustine's work, and through his influence, efforts were made to restore a worthy state of preaching.

Alcuin put together a homilary, or a collection of homilies, for use by parish priests who had limited training and resources. He and his colleagues made a lasting contribution in bringing British and Anglo-Saxon theological works into the Carolingian reforms. They revised the lectionary of the church and established an order for the church year. This church calendar has remained essentially unchanged among Roman Catholics, Lutherans, and Anglicans.

Another notable homilary was that by Hrabanus Maurus (776?–856), a pupil of Alcuin, who later also became an archbishop of Mainz.[3]

After A.D. 1000, the church, amidst polity and theological disputes, needed a rallying point to pull it together and to move it on its mission. It found just that, when the Holy Land fell into the hands of the wandering Seljuk Turks. Until the eleventh century, although Jerusalem was controlled by Moslems, Christians had been allowed to make pilgrimages there and even to maintain their churches. The Turks, however, were a fierce people and began to persecute the Christians. As a result, Pope Urban I appealed to a synod at

Clermont in France in November 1095, in a sermon so stirring that the congregation reportedly cried out "God wills it," and this became the slogan of the campaign to free the Holy City. Great preaching missions were mounted to gather forces for the Crusades, and two especially notable preachers emerged: Peter the Hermit and Bernard of Clairvaux.

Peter of Amiens, or the Hermit (1050?–1115), rallied members for the First Crusade, which began in 1096. He was a very small, ungainly fellow, whose speaking was made powerful by his fiery enthusiasm and great flow of words. Doubtless a fanatic, he appealed to the spirit of adventure and the love of war, often striking his chest with a heavy crucifix, drawing blood, and then shedding torrents of tears before the cross. His exceptional eloquence is reported to have had an overpowering effect on persons of both high and low estate.

Bernard of Clairvaux (1091–1153) was involved with the Second Crusade. He was a pious Cistercian monk, born of noble parents, who first had decided to become a knight but then had surrendered to the call of monastic life. His commanding leadership and eloquence brought recruits and wealth to the Cistercian order, and he became an important man of affairs in both church and government—a real power behind the emperor and the pope. He gave himself time to master the techniques of sermon preparation and became probably the most effective preacher of his century. When he preached, monks from the monasteries and huge crowds from the cities pressed to hear him. Witnesses reported that he made a gripping impression—even on those who did not understand his language. He was one of the first to break the pattern of plagiarizing patristic sermons, and his homilies addressed to the monks of Clairvaux are among the most touching and exquisite documents of this kind from the Middle Ages. He loved to preach, and we are told that he preached much more often than required by the rules of his order.

The Crusades, continuing into the thirteenth century, greatly stirred the heart of a fragmented Europe and drew it together against the common enemy. Although they finally failed in their purpose, the Crusades were one of the major factors in leading Europe out of the disarray of the Dark Ages. Since the conflict was far away in the Holy Land, there was relative peace at home; feudal nobles had less time and money to disturb the homeland with local wars. Economic conditions improved and encouraged the rise of a middle class, which in turn resulted in more cultural activity throughout all society.[4] A vast trade developed between Europe and the Orient, contributing to prosperity and the regrowth of cities, and this led to the decline of serfdom.

One further important event should be mentioned before we move beyond the early Middle Ages. In 1054, the church split into a western, or Roman Catholic Church, which acknowleged the pope as Christ's supreme vicar on earth, and the Eastern Orthodox Churches, which recognized the patriarch of Constantinople as the preeminent ecclesiastical figure. Since our concern is to trace the heritage of American preaching, only incidental further mention will be made of the eastern church. Christianity came to America primarily through the influence of the Roman Catholic and the reformed churches of the western world.

The medieval church contributed much good to the daily life of the people: It was often a social center, a school, and a meeting place, and church attendance was in part a social occasion. There was only one church and everyone belonged to it. It became very powerful over the years, and sometimes the pope had more wealth and power than all the kings and nobles combined. There were, however, times when he had little power. Some popes were competent men; some were not; but all influenced the secular rulers of their times. There were many contests for political power between the church and the governments. The great princes of the church were part of the feudal system, and bishops and archbishops were often vassals of lords and kings; many bishops were nobles who did not have a true calling but were appointed for political and financial reasons.

Monks and nuns were honored members of the population. The monasteries were held in high regard, and rightly so. Had it not been for the industrious and scholarly monks, much of the Greek and Roman learning might have been lost. The monks also helped educate children; they preserved crafts and skills and taught them to their people; and especially between the sixth and eleventh centuries when Europe was in chaos and confusion, the monks brought order to many communities.

But preaching itself was greatly neglected, and over wide areas and through long years there was almost no preaching at all.

Sermonizing became primarily a function of the bishops, since the educational level of the priests hardly permitted competent scriptural exposition. Unfortunately, the education of the bishops also often left something to be desired and they, too, sometimes came to rely heavily on sermons of the church Fathers and those of such men as Pope Gregory the Great (540–604). Gregory's series of homilies was used extensively for centuries, and he exerted great influence in doctrinal and liturgical matters. The more ambitious preacher/priests searched Augustine and Origen and other Fathers for sermon materials, but the majority of the simple parish priests did not have the training or library resources to do the research necessary for original sermon construction.

Sermons were preached primarily in monastery chapels rather than in the parish churches, where worship was mainly liturgical. When the common people gathered in church, it was usually to witness ceremonies and to listen to chanting and intoning. Sermons, when given, were most often in Latin, a language few understood, even in Italy. Most of those who preached in the vernacular presented eulogies to the saints or accounts of current miracles rather than focusing on the Savior and the simple kerygma.

The preachers of the Middle Ages took over Origen's method of allegorical interpretation from the ancient church and then carried it a step further. Preachers of the time were expected to have seven or eight interpretations of any particular scriptural passage, often confusing and confounding even the simplest of texts. Preaching was far removed from daily life.

But there were glimmers of hope. Bishop Theodulf of Orleans, an ecclesiastical scholar and one of the cultured leaders in the Carolingian renaissance, told his clergy in the year 797, "He who knows the scripture may proclaim [preach the scripture]; he who does not know it may at least communicate to the people what is most known that they may avoid the bad and do the good, seek peace and pursue it."[5] At Tours and Rheims in 813, and at Mainz in 846, church councils decreed that bishops should preach homilies in the vernacular.

The Carolingian reform period marked the beginning of a practice of using the traditional simple homily. There are cases reported where the bishops of this period exhorted their clergy to explain the gospel through the homilies and to add some simple information on the faith and morals of Christianity by teaching the lay people the Creed, the Ave Maria, and other texts of Scripture in the vernacular. This was at least a beginning toward the restoration of preaching the kerygma; it was the initial stage of the time of recovery, which would be demonstrated more fully in the eleventh and twelfth centuries with the establishment of the preaching orders.

The three centuries immediately prior to the Reformation saw a major renewal of emphasis on preaching throughout the western world. The Fourth Lateran Council of the Christian Church in 1215 urged that parish priests preach in the vernacular to their people, and the time was noted for an increase in the frequency of preaching, the development of homiletic aids, many preaching manuals, and collections of sermons. One of the best known works on sermon construction, the *Summa Praedicantium*, was the work of English Dominican Johannes de Bromyard in the fourteenth century. It was printed at least twice before the Reformation and, like many other works of its time, was a dictionary of topics, illustrations, and the like, that a preacher might use in constructing original sermons.

BEGINNINGS OF PREACHING RENEWAL

The thirteenth century witnessed a genuine beginning of renewal in preaching. Concomitant with the Lateran Council in 1215 came the establishment of two preaching orders: the Preaching Brothers of Dominic (1170–1221) and the Brothers of the Poor of Francis of Assisi (1182–1226). The two orders arose simultaneously in different parts of Europe—the Dominicans in southern France in 1215 and the Franciscans in Italy in 1209. Dominic's order was established for the purpose of converting heretics by preaching truth; Francis' order was established as a reform movement, opposed to the wealth, luxury, and impurity of existing monasteries and committed to establishing new parishes in urban areas. Both orders were developed at a time when it was recognized that there was a need for preaching to deal with corrupt conditions in church and society. Both men recognized that the demands of preaching required a commitment of time, which should not be imposed upon by other matters that occupied the energies of the parish clergy. Although both orders followed monastic rules, bound by vows of chastity, poverty, and obedience, they did not cloister themselves, but worked with and among their people.

Both groups were given freedom to preach in any parish, and through their influence a great rebirth of popular preaching took place throughout the west. Large crowds gathered to hear the friars, and outdoor sermons became regular practice. The Dominicans, especially, were thoroughly trained in the best homiletic tradition based on thorough classical rhetorial principles.

The wandering friars, all of whom were designated as preaching specialists, often drew large crowds for sermons at special assemblies, in contrast to the usual liturgical mass. Feast and fast occasions, then, became the special preaching seasons, which in turn led to a lesser emphasis on the sermon at the regular mass. Thus there came to be something of a competition and cleavage between liturgy and preaching—between ritual and the spoken word—much to the detriment of both.[6]

The Franciscans and the Dominicans made significant contributions to preaching theory and practice; they preached when little preaching was being done and when little development of the art was taking place. The two leaders must have been exceptional preachers themselves. Francis taught by example; his preaching is reported to have been quiet and conversational. By contrast, Dominic was known as a preacher of unusual force and fervor. Above all, both aimed at being effective proclaimers of the Word. But since the friars did not serve in pastoral situations, the relevance of their preaching to a particular circumstance was limited, and they did not serve to bring about the return of effective preaching to the parish priesthood of most congregations.

The philosophy of the itinerant preachers was expressed some thirty years after the founding of the Dominican order by Humbert de Romans, who was then director general of the order. Explaining that although the laity understood nothing of the Latin liturgy, they could understand the sermon, and hence by preaching, God is glorified in a clearer and more open manner than by any other act of worship. He set forth a definitive treatise on the preparation and delivery of sermons and noted that "the talent for preaching is obtained through the special gift of God, yet the wise preacher will do his own part of the work, and diligently study that he may preach correctly."[7]

Anthony of Padua (1195–1231) was one of the best known of the Franciscan friars. He was a missionary to Africa and later to Italy, where he gained a strong reputation. Sometimes thirty thousand people came to hear him, and it is reported that on occasion, as many as twenty thousand waited all night before a platform where he was to preach the next day. Fortunately, many of his sermons, or at least briefs of them, still exist. They were published, we are told, for the benefit of other preachers. He also left the first collection of what we now would call "snappy sermon-starters." He was careful to divide his sermons into several sections, following Aristotelian logic, probably in an effort to make them more acceptable to the rational mind of his day. He was particularly adept at drawing illustrations from the lives of the people, from nature, and from animals, in contrast to the usual tendency of that time to illustrate from the lives of the saints and martyrs.

Thomas Aquinas (1225?–1274), in his brief life, became probably the greatest theologian of the Middle Ages and one of the greatest minds in the history of philosophy. He was a simple Italian Dominican friar, popular with the common people. But he was also a profound theologian/philosopher and was often called the Angelic Doctor, and Prince of Scholastics. His sermons were not generally imaginative or flowing, but he was skilled at using homely and lively comparisons, for explanation as well as for argument.

Several other outstanding preachers of the time should be recognized. The mystical sermon was popularized by Meister Eckhart (1260–1327) and Johannes Tauler (1266–1367), both German Dominican theologians, mystics, and preachers; by Heinrich Suso (1295–1366), a German mystic itinerant preacher; and later, by Jean de Gerson (1363–1429), a French theologian.

What we now would call the evangelistic or revival sermon was used extensively by Vincent Ferrer (1359–1419), renowned itinerant Spanish Dominican; and by two Italian Franciscans, John Capistrano (1386–1456) and Bernardino of Siena (1380–1444), who were especially well known as effective preachers.

As the Middle Ages drew nearer to the Age of the Renaissance, reform preaching came to the fore, especially in the work of Englishman John Wycliffe (1320?-1384), later to be called the Morning Star of the Reformation; John Huss (1369–1415), a Bohemian religious reformer influenced by Wycliffe's writing; and Girolamo Savonarola (1452–1498), an Italian Dominican reformer. Clearly this period of church history was blessed with preachers as no time had been since the patristic era. (Note, however, that the Fifth Lateran Council, 1516, suggested that much of the preaching emphasis had been devoted to superstition rather than to the kerygma or evangelical gospel.)[8]

John Wycliffe had strong views about almost everything, including preaching. He became a severe critic of the Franciscans, but at the same time emulated much of their idealism in his own preaching and taught it to his Lollard followers. Wycliffe regarded the apostolic period as the golden age of the church and preaching, and he was diligent in seeking to prove that preaching was more important than the Eucharist. Nevertheless, it was fundamental to his eucharistic theology that the body of Christ is in the consecrated host. Protestants should not take Wycliffe's emphasis on preaching out of proportion to his intent; much of his enthusiasm grew out of his concern for the poor peasants of England and his desire to share the gospel with them in an intelligible and relevant way. He trained his "poor priests" to preach simply, and directly to the needs of the poor.

Wycliffe became the mightiest champion of the new doctrine of the primacy of preaching. This fiery churchman, by precept and example, held that only a sermon in the mother tongue of the people is truly edifying, and his translation of the Bible into the vernacular further confirms his deep concern for preaching the gospel to the common people of his homeland. The immediate effects of his activities were limited, but he anticipated a time when the ministry of the Word was to come into its own.

After Wycliffe, came an Italian—another Dominican preacher who must be mentioned—Savonarola (1452–1498). His emphasis was on the prophetic, and in him we see a striking comparison to the Hebrew prophets; he seemed to have a profound consciousness of being a messenger of God. He denounced in vehement sermons the corruption in secular life and in the ruling class, and the worldliness of the clergy. He dared to censure Pope Alexander VI, was excommunicated, and eventually tortured, hanged, and burned. Rarely, if ever, has the spoken word of a man exercised such influence in the Christian church, despite the fact that he was not a great expositor. His star shone brightly for a time but, perhaps because of his prophetic urgency, he did not have a great influence on later developments in Christian preaching.

In retrospect, we can see that during the thousand years we call the Middle Ages, despite setbacks of every sort, the true Christian faith was never extinguished and shows itself in recurring outbursts of evangelical witness and in earnest efforts at reform. Ultimately, this gave rise to the purifying dialogue and debate of the Protestant Reformation, releasing forces of reform in the church and calling the entire church back to the kerygma and evangelical witness.

THE RENEWAL OF PREACHING

On October 31, 1517, a burly, brusque, extroversive German Catholic monk named Martin Luther nailed a list of ninety-five theses on the Castle Church door at Wittenberg. Those theses affirmed that Luther would be glad to debate anyone who wished to argue for the church's practice of selling indulgences. He little knew where this action would lead him.

Unquestionably, Luther was a Catholic seeking to reform his church, as had scores of others before him. He wanted to purify the church, not to divide or destroy it. And while his actions led to schism, many Catholics are beginning to view him not so much as a Protestant, but as a Catholic Reformer who was so hardheaded that he sacrificed unity for truth.

News of the theses ultimately reached Rome, where Pope Leo X dismissed them as a mere squabble among monks, even suggesting that Luther was simply drunk: "He will think differently when he is sober." But by 1520, when it had become apparent that Luther's teaching threatened to destroy the whole structure of clerical and papal control, Leo thought differently and drafted a sentence of excommunication in the form of a call to arms: "Arise, O, Lord, and judge thy cause. A wild boar has invaded thy vineyard. . . . We can no longer suffer the serpent to creep through the field of the Lord."

Luther was banned from the empire, his followers were condemned, and his books were ordered to be eradicated from the memory of man.[9]

Some years before, when Luther had been a student at Wittenberg, he wrote to his mother that God's Word teaches us to trust only in Jesus Christ. The full impact of that doctrine of grace and justification by faith enveloped him slowly. The Sacrament of the Eucharist had been to Luther the foundation from which there was no appeal; it was the literal Body of Christ. When he rejected the Mass it became quite necessary for him to replace it with some other "ultimate foundation" of authority. That something was the Word of God, as made alive in the Bible, and as made alive in preaching.

Luther did not sweep away the sacraments; he wanted not to destroy the liturgy of the church but to reinvest it with an awareness of the dominance of the living Word. To him the preaching of the Word was the Word of God. This did not mean that the living Word was simply the act of preaching or the act of reading the Scriptures in the vernacular. It meant the discovery of the living God in the interaction of the listener/reader and the spoken/written words about God.

For Luther, the living Word worked most actively when it was preached from the pulpit by a man standing solidly on biblical truths. This was in no sense idolatry of preaching or of the Bible; he did not believe that preaching, in and of itself, or even the Bible, were of inherent divine merit. Somehow he came upon the notion that the Bible and preaching form that point of contact—that bodyless intersection—where the divine and human meet. God is still All-in-all and man is still in need of the redemptive acts of the Father. He was convinced that God could not be put under indulgence obligation or coercion by any man; the forgiveness God extends is an act of pure grace—a gift freely offered to all who respond in trust to the invitation and promise. This was Luther's basic idea, and that of the Reformers, and as they came to discover this nature of the Christian faith, they rediscovered the nature of the church—the church as God's people, the whole body of the faithful of God in Christ.

Luther insisted that the sermon must be central in worship. Other items in the service need not be diminished in importance but could be fulfilled as the sermon brought the living Word to illuminate those items for the participating congregation. To Luther, faith was not found only through preaching, but it was therein perfected. Note his exposition of Galatians: "As God at first gives faith through the word, so he hereafter also exercises, increases, confirms, and perfects it through the word." Therefore, the worship of God at its best, and the finest keeping of the Sabbath, consisted of exercising oneself in piety and in proclaiming and hearing the Word.[10] This theology of preaching was radical for Luther's day, though it was substantially the same point of view offered by Wycliffe a century and a half earlier.

Luther's critique of the established church led to schism in both church and political state. Confusion, and often chaos, resulted, especially in relation to the disposition of emptied monastic cloisters and their properties. The "freedom" of Protestantism generated new and different liturgical forms in almost every village, often without regard to decorum and decency. Was not each man a priest now? Who is to perform the sacraments? Might not any man solemnize marriages? To deal with the vacuum of structure and authority, Luther turned temporarily to sympathetic German princes who, as emergency bishops, took charge of stabilizing not only church organization but church properties as well. This temporary appeal to the princes resulted in the emergence of Luther's movement as the official church in Germany, a position it still occupies.

A few years later in Geneva, John Calvin (1509–1564) led a church-reform movement that received considerably less pressure and interference from the established government. As mentor of the Reformed tradition, he became a great expositor—perhaps the greatest in the history of the church since John Chrysostom. To him, the written Word and its exposition through preaching were paramount; nevertheless, the Word without the Sacrament was incomplete, truncated, aborted, and did not reach its proper fulfillment. The Sacraments, according to Calvin, are seals of the divine Word; they carry into the senses what has been thought or conceived by the heart and mind. They are preaching, carried a step beyond itself, so that it addresses the whole of our being.[11]

Calvin seemed quite intent on expounding the entire Bible in sermons. Apparently, he preached through the books of Scripture in continuous order—Old Testament as well as New—and from his time, use of the Old Testament has taken on increased importance in Reformed preaching.

The outcome of the Reformation in England was much the same as in Germany and Switzerland, except that the initiative was taken by the king rather than the church. And since the English monarchs were able to command the cooperation of the majority of the bishops, church properties, church order, the parish and the diocese were basically unchanged except in name: They simply were called Church of England rather than Roman Catholic.

Fundamental to the Church of England as the established church was the principle of royal supremacy argued by King Henry VIII, in his thrust to restructure the church in his country. He maintained the divine right of kings, as opposed to the divine right of popes, calling for joint royal sovereignty over state and church.

As early as 1540, Thomas Cranmer (1489–1556), Archbishop of Canterbury from 1553 until deposed by the accession of Queen Mary, supported the divine right of kings doctrine. "All Christian princes have committed unto them immediately of God the whole cure of all their subjects as well concerning the admission of God's word for the cure of souls as concerning the ministration of things political and civil governance."[12] This placed church offices at the disposal of the royal government, a condition lending itself to possible abuse in the appointment of clergy. Cranmer eventually was condemned for treason, convicted by a papal commission (1555), excommunicated by the Roman Catholic Church, condemned for heresy, and burned at the stake.

Growing out of what came to be called the Protestant Reformation are three major ecclesiastical traditions: Lutheran, Anglican, and Reformed. Other major Protestant bodies, including Congregationalists, Baptists, Methodists, and Disciples, are essentially post-Reformation in origin. They came into being not as products of any marked theological debate, but out of differences of opinion on the meaning of church polity. The Reformers had emphasized the nature of the church as a people of God and had insisted that faith and trust be placed in Jesus Christ rather than in the clergy or the church. Thus it became necessary to remodel the ecclesiastical structure so that it could express adequately and accurately the new understanding of the meaning of the church.

As we look back on the Reformation, it is easy to see that two strains of Protestantism developed—right and left wings. The right-wing churches were established as state churches in western Europe, where Protestantism gained the upper hand. They included Lutheran and Reformed churches, which were established as the state religions in all the Protestant German states; in the Protestant cantons of Switzerland; in the Scandinavian countries of Denmark, Norway, and Sweden; and in Holland. In the British Isles the Presbyterian church was established in Scotland; in England, the Church of England became the official religion. These right-wing churches were liturgical, confessional churches, refusing to break entirely with the tradition and heritage of the Roman church. They drew creeds and confessions and adopted much of the theology that had developed through the centuries of Christianity, with the exception of the penitential system of the late medieval church.

On the other hand, the radical left-wing type of Protestantism grew mainly from the common folk of the Palatine Germans in southwest Germany and Switzerland. Leaders of the left-wing groups were not as well known as were Luther, Calvin, and Zwingli (1484–1531). These churches rejected many things from Christian tradition that were accepted by the right-wing churches, and they insisted that the Reformation be carried to its logical conclusion. To them, religion was an intensely personal inner experience with minimal institutional involvement. They placed little emphasis, if any, on creeds and sacraments, but supreme importance upon teaching and preaching.

The left-wing phase of the Reformation gradually spread into other Protestant lands where there was some dissatisfaction with the nature of the reforms that had been adopted. Adherents rejected state churches and denied civil authority the right to interfere in any matter of conscience. Essentially nonliturgical, they gave minimal credence to the sacraments. Some even refused to use the word sacraments, preferring instead, "ordinances," or "religious exercises." In deemphasizing the sacraments they necessarily devoted great attention to the development of linguistic communication through teaching and preaching. With this thrust, the left-wing free churches have developed a disproportionately large number of noted preachers, as compared to the liturgical right-wing branch of Protestantism.

Left-wing Protestants were banned in much of Europe and the British Isles during the Reformation period and generally until the mid-seventeenth century. This condition would later make serious-minded religionists uncomfortable enough to seek refuge elsewhere—a situation which spurred many to seek their fortunes and religious freedom in the New World. Left-wing Protestantism would find fertile soil in America. Even in this day, the nonestablished churches on the continent and in England are often held in rather low esteem.

A major factor giving impetus to the birth of the Reformation was the period of general revival of learning called the Renaissance, beginning during the time of the Crusades and extending into the early seventeenth century. One of the most important phenomena of the Renaissance was the gradual change in attitude toward men and women as persons. Increasingly, the person was perceived to have inherent worth and dignity, a concept of major importance to Martin Luther.

The Renaissance began in Italy and spread gradually to other parts of Europe. In Italy it made for a renewal of interest in the arts; but as it made its way northward, the emphasis was on more serious things. The people in Germany, Holland, England, and Sweden were particularly conscious of their eternal souls and did not make light of things they considered holy. They were interested in the renewal of the study of the ancient philosphers. And so the church, representing serious and somber topics, was affected by the Renaissance. In contrast, the papacy and the College of Cardinals had for generations been almost exclusively Italian, with strong interest in the pleasanter topics of the Renaissance such as music, art, and theater. This underlying orientation of the northern and southern parts of Europe was a major factor in the development of the Reformation, which grew rather naturally as a product of the northern section.

Again, the political situation in Europe helped to generate and extend the religious revolt. Many of the local rulers wanted independence from papal authority and freedom from the heavy taxation of the Holy Roman Empire. Tradesmen and peasants were seeking more and more rights from rulers whom they felt were supported by the church. Luther's challenge to the church thus became a rallying point for several widely differing groups, from princes to peasants, who hailed him as their own special kind of hero, and it became apparent that discontent was rather widespread in the upper reaches of the empire. When Luther was handed the not unexpected papal bull denouncing him, dated June 15, 1520, he promptly and publicly burned it, amid great acclaim from his followers.

Other notable scholars helped to spread the Reformation. Luther had been greatly influenced by the ideas of Wycliffe and John Huss. His doctrine of justification by faith was based to some extent on his study of Johannes Tauler's development of the mystic idea of heart religion. Philipp Melanchthon (1497–1560), professor of Greek and theology and one of Luther's colleagues at the University of Wittenberg, was chief theologian of the movement in Germany. His moderation served to temper Luther's vehemence, and he later drafted the Augsburg Confession, still a primary document in Lutheranism. Erasmus (1466?–1536), the great Dutch theologian and thinker, and a scholar of Greek and patristic philosophy, at first favored the Reformation but later opposed it and attempted to promote reforms within the Roman Catholic Church. Zwingli in Switzerland, John Colet in England, and John Calvin—all were prominent thinkers giving support to the movement.

But it was Luther's public challenge of painful religious doctrine that activated the far-reaching ferment—political, economic, philosophical, and religious. By 1530 so many things had occurred that the Reformation got out of hand, well beyond even Luther's control.

The fact that in the mid-fifteenth century the printing press had been invented in Germany and was more widely used in that country than in others, contributed to the distribution of tracts and books and scriptures, all of which fed the growing controversy. Indeed, the Bible, with the advent of the printing press, was no longer a mysterious manuscript owned and explained only by the church. It became a household Book, and as families began to read it, they discovered concepts somewhat different from many ideas they had learned secondhand from the church. So people began to ask questions—questions that could not be easily answered—and this, too, laid some of the foundation for the acceptance of Reformation ideas.

The papacy and most Roman Catholic clergymen were naturally shocked and incensed by the events centering in the University of Wittenberg. As the reform movement spread it threatened the very existence of the Roman church in large segments of the world, and Counter-Reformation sentiments and activities swept through the land. A representative, if not typical example of this reaction occurred when Ignatius Loyola (1491–1556), formerly a military man, and seven other students from the Sorbonne founded a fraternity, mutually pledging to lead holy lives and to devote themselves to the service of the church. Just a few years later, after much growth and success, this group was recognized as the Society of Jesus, now called Jesuits. They were originally a militarily organized, disciplined, obedient, committed order of priests, dedicatd to education and preaching efforts to reclaim Protestants for the true faith and to convert infidels.

Ecclesiastical response to the Reformation motivated the formation of the Council of Trent, which met episodically from 1545 to 1563. The council worked unsuccessfully to effect a political solution to the Reformation. It was able to tighten and clarify doctrine and discipline, and this led to a succession of able popes during the second half of the sixteenth century—popes who were interested less in the art forms of the Renaissance than in the faith of the church. Luther and Calvin, however, had challenged too much that was fundamental to the nature of Roman Catholicism as then understood, and the council was forced to accept the split in the church. It could not be healed at that time without radical departure from traditional church practice.

In retrospect, it is clear that in most cases the attitude of the prince, or the head of the secular government in a particular locale, was the deciding factor in the success or failure of reform efforts in the church of the area. When the king or prince was in favor of Catholicism, the country or state generally remained Catholic; when he sided with the Reformers, the area became Protestant. In this way the unity of the western church was broken. A full century after 1517, princes and popes and people and philosophers and preachers and priests and bishops and laymen still debated and jockeyed and fought and persecuted one another—Protestant against Catholic, Catholic against Protestant—until 1618, when open warfare began the Thirty Years' War. During the ensuing years, that war engulfed essentially all Europe at one time or another.

The story of Reformation and Counter-Reformation is not a pretty one for either Protestants or Catholics. No one emerged with clean hands, except perhaps some of the pacifists and Pietists of the left-wing Reformers; strange and ugly events took place in the name of religion. Heretics were burned at the stake, sometimes after a trial. Heresies were searched out in all areas, as in the case of the scientist Galileo (1564–1642), who was tried by the Inquisition and forced to deny his belief that the sun is the celestial body around which earth and planets revolve. Protestant leaders in Holland and France were killed; William of Orange was murdered; the great Armada was sunk; and Catholic Queen Mary of Scots was beheaded. The Edict of Toleration of Nantes was passed and later rejected.

Then in 1648 at Westphalia, a treaty was signed ending the war. The lines were still drawn; the Catholic powers remained Catholic and the Protestant powers remained Protestant. The Swiss and Dutch Protestants were recognized as independent republics; the Holy Roman Empire continued only as a shadow entity. But apparently some good was accomplished, for both Catholic and Protestant have been discouraged from entering into the same kind of nonsense again. They left one another in peace, agreeing to disagree. Now the Protestants were free to quibble with one another, and that is precisely what they began to do in earnest, once they settled down in the New World.

III. PREACHING: AMERICA—TO 1900

COLONIAL AMERICA

A brief work of this sort cannot trace with any detail the flow of preaching through Reformation/Counter-Reformation in western Europe and the British Isles. Further, since we are interested in a uniquely American perspective of Christian preaching, we shall touch only ever so lightly on events between the Protestant Reformation and the British settling of our Eastern Seaboard. This colonization, among other things, was basically a Puritan exodus from a threatening and unsettled ecclesiastical climate in England, and later in western Europe.

England under Henry VIII (ruled 1509–1547) *seemed* to slip easily through the Reformation to the newly established Anglican religion. However, King Henry had underestimated the forces that would be let loose when he dislodged Roman Catholicism in his country and claimed the church for his very own. Indeed, he set off what was clearly the longest and most turbulent Reformation in all Christendom. In one of its several definitive stages, anti-Puritan William Laud was appointed Archbishop of Canterbury. His church policies sent swarms of English Puritans fleeing from British shores, many of them ultimately to find haven in New England. But this event gets ahead of our story.

The earliest colonists in America arrived in 1540 in New Mexico and in 1577 in Florida, well antedating the settlement of Jamestown in 1607 and Plymouth in 1620. But it was at Plymouth, and soon afterward in the Boston Bay Colony, that preaching in the American tradition began—preaching that was to be a potent tool, religiously and politically, for generations.

The Spanish colonists in Florida and New Mexico were not of the sort of cultural orientation that led to a desire for political and religious freedom. And the colonists in Virginia were businessmen; they came to make a fortune, not to make a life. But the New England colonists, on the other hand, came to settle, to build lives, and to establish a new Zion in the wilderness. They came bringing their entire culture with them, including their preachers, who were as important as any other necessity in their tightly knit little world.

The religious controversies in western Europe, and especially in England at the outset of colonization in New England, precipitated the exodus of Puritans and Nonconformists from England and Ireland, and later from Scotland and western Europe. Colonization at the outset was almost exclusively English and primarily Protestant—of the Puritan Nonconformist variety. John Cotton (1584–1652), Puritan teaching elder and minister of the church in Boston from 1635 until 1652, is representative of the type and caliber of ministry in early New England. He had held a distinguished pastorate in England for some twenty years and had been identified as somewhat liberal, stressing the volition of man in religious matters, almost to the point of free will. Something happened to his thinking, however, before he arrived at his Boston pulpit. There he became severe, strict, and absolute in preaching the sovereignty of God and the complete helplessness of humanity in seeking a saving relationship with God. He preached a doctrine of limited grace; salvation could not be earned—it was a free gift of God for the elect. His sermons were generally characterized by simplicity and directness; his language was geared to the humblest of his parishioners. He preached with quiet dignity, but with a forceful emphasis.[1]

In most cases in the early New England colonial village, the minister was the effective leader of the community. New settlements invariably built a church and obtained a clergyman. John Cotton wrote home to England that there was "nothing cheap in New England but milk and ministers."[2]

The church, or the meeting house, was the hub of the village. The pulpit was central in the service. The ministers were men of quality, often from among the best of society in England. John Cotton, Thomas Hooker (1586?–1647), and John Davenport (1597–1670), all Cambridge and Oxford graduates and ministers in the first generation of colonists, were invited to sit in the Westminster Assembly in London. Generally, the minister was a man of affairs, interested in and participating in everything of general concern to the community. Many were students who studied rigorously, and most were also farmers or craftsmen. The minister was the "person," or parson, the best educated, wisest man of the town. He enjoyed an assured social position and exercised a strong voice in civil affairs. He was held in high esteem for good reason, and the community turned to him for spiritual, personal, political, and civil advice. He was a worthy man.

Things were quite different in Boston in 1640 from the way they had been in London, or Glasgow, or Leyden before immigration, only a few months before. The minister was viewed as a messenger of God, a guide to help his people know God's will for their lives in the New Canaan. He was expected to counsel concerning families, epidemics, and civil strife, in addition to providing spiritual nurture.

We have been led to believe that most of the sermons of those worthy gentlemen were of goodly length—up to three hours on occasion. Certainly some must have been, but we find that many of Cotton's sermons could easily have been preached in thirty minutes. Typically, they were doctrinal lectures such as one might hear in a theological classroom, usually of abstract exposition and analysis of philosophical and theological topics. Occasionally specific sins were touched upon, as when "Mr. Williams preached against veils and Mr. Elliott denounced wigs, long hair, and tobacco."[3]

From the very beginning, church life in America was considerably different from that in England and Europe because of the nature of the laity. A natural selection process had motivated a certain type of person to risk life in the New World. The people who made the choice to come were necessarily brave souls and inherently individualistic. The challenge of the experience and the pride of the survivors worked to reinforce character and courage. Thus by and large, the colonists were Puritans whose inner strength stressed individualism; they worked for congregational autonomy in their churches. Even in the central and southern colonies where Anglicanism was predominant, the power of the laity was strong. The vestry of those parishes usually controlled the churches with a firm hand and even, on occasion, refused to accept a minister sent by a bishop.

Conditions in western Europe toward the end of the seventeenth century, bolstered by news of the opportunties in the new land, furthered migrations of left-wing Protestants, particularly of the Anabaptist tradition. The primary ethnic origins of these people were French (Huguenot), German, and Scotch-Irish. Before 1690 the population was predominantly of English Puritan heritage, but following that period, Mennonites, Dunkards, Schwenkfelders, Moravians, and others contributed to the shifting ratio of denominations. Naturally this affected the character of religion, since these left-wing Protestants stressed the rights and privileges of the common man, and it brought forth preaching that emphasized personal religion as a condition of the heart and of the inward person, rather than of forms, creeds, and confessions.

In the early part of the eighteenth century new waves of Scotch-Irish immigration began. Most of the people were radically Protestant, mainly Presbyterian, and all avidly supported a free church as opposed to a state church. This, too, had its impact on preaching. No matter what happens, the state church is funded as long as the state is solvent. The free church is funded only if the ministry can motivate the parishioners voluntarily to support it. This is considerably different from a tax-supported state church which is, in theory, composed of all citizens of the society in which it operates. The voluntarism of the free church provides an added motivation for the minister to be persuasive in his pulpit duties. The Scotch-Irish Presbyterians were especially urgent in demanding a free chuch arrangement.

The church and its preaching were also affected at this time by the "natural rights" writings of John Locke (1632–1704), English philosopher/statesman. His two *Treatises on Government* (1690), *The Reasonableness of Christianity as Delivered in the Scriptures* (1695), and his four *Letters on Toleration* (1689–1706), argued persuasively for separation of church and state and for a free church in a free state—a state that is sanctioned by the citizens, who voluntarily surrender some of their natural rights for the common good of society.

Hence, since the people were bent in the individualistic, pioneering, self-reliant direction, they tended to listen with favor only to rhetoric, religious as well as political, supportive of that orientation. This general frame of the popular mind was further encouraged by the religious revivals that began to sweep over the colonies in the mid-1720s and continued, at various levels of intensity, into the Revolutionary period.

Conditions for Roman Catholics in the British colonies in America were not even tolerable, except in Maryland (for a time), Pennsylania, Rhode Island, and New Jersey. In the other colonies Catholics were hated intruders, subject to various legal and nonlegal harassments. Even in Maryland, founded by Catholic Lord Calvert, Anglicanism was adopted as the official religion in 1702, and laws were passed forbidding Catholic priests to say mass in the province. Under the same law, parents could be fined £100 for sending their children abroad for a Catholic education. Happily, this law was not well received even among Protestants, and it was repealed in time.

The militant anti-Catholic sentiments were holdovers from the not yet settled embers of the Reformation/Counter-Reformation controversy in Europe. In fact, in England the controversy was still quite heated. The English had a difficult time deciding whether to allow Catholic monarchs to reign in their land and assume leadership of the Church of England. In the colonies the basic task for Catholics was to gain a foothold of respectability and to meld the parish members from diverse geographical and language backgrounds into some semblance of unity. The few priests who were then available worked primarily, of necessity, at church management and eccleiastical housekeeping chores, as opposed to engaging in missionary and evangelistic efforts. The Jesuits, under difficult conditions, were an exception; they found some time and resources to work among the Indians in and around Pennsylvania and Maryland. It was not until the American Revolution that a new day of religious freedom would permit Roman Catholics to live, worship, work, and preach freely.

THE GREAT AWAKENING

Theodore Jacob Frelinghuysen (1691–1748), a German Pietist pastor, came to the colonies in 1720 to serve three congregations of Dutch settlers in the Raritan Valley of New Jersey. He was not the kind of minister his parishioners had expected. They wanted someone to lead them through the motions of religion, not the emotions of it. But Frelinghuysen preached an "inner experience" religion and sought to bring about conversions. Naturally there was controversy. The young and poor generally supported him; the upper classes and well-to-do were distressed. Soon, however, a general revival among his congregation resulted, and we now refer to it as the earliest stage of what came to be called the First Great Awakening.

Across the Delaware River at Neshaminy in Pennsylvania, an evangelical Presbyterian minister, William Tennent, established a small school to educate his own sons. Others desired schooling, and so Tennent erected a small log building where he taught young men aspiring to the Presbyterian ministry. Critics derided the "log college," but this little school eventually led to the establishment of Princeton University and also to a succession of other log colleges operated by Presbyterian ministers as they followed the advancing frontier in colonial America.

Back in New Jersey, Frelinghuysen faced stiff opposition not only from within his own church but from other Dutch ministers in nearby New York City. Nevertheless, he continued his work, with frequent conversions even among his elders, deacons, and former opponents. The revival reached its peak in 1726 with a large ingathering of new members and the spreading of the spirit of revivalism to other nearby Dutch Reformed churches. Gilbert Tennent (1703–1764), a son of William and a recent student at the log college, was called about this time to be minister of the Presbyterian church in New Brunswick, New Jersey. He joined Frelinghuysen in his work to promote revivalism in central New Jersey, where conditions were ripe for spiritual renewal.

The situation in New England was different from that in New Jersey, but the people there were ready for revival. The first generation of Puritans in New England constituted only about 10 percent of the population, but dominated the culture. Oddly enough, only one-fourth of the children of the first generation became active church members. By the end of the first decade of the eighteenth century, only 5 percent of the people in America belonged to churches, and extremely low moral conditions prevailed. At this time also, there was a large influx of Europeans moving into new regions where the old ways of organized religion did not fit. Some system was needed to reach these newcomers who were essentially free from church connections and from the conserving restraints of community life of the Old World.

Thus it was that the office of the itinerant evangelist came into being to meet contemporary conditions. As noted earlier, the revivals stressed Pietism, or the inward experience of religion, as opposed to the systematic analysis of religious ideas of the Calvinists. However, when Calvinism was applied to individuals, it adopted the approach of Pietism and was surprisingly effective in reaching and touching as the revivalists stressed the equality of all persons in the sight of God.

Some eight years after the peak of the Raritan Valley revival, unusual responses to the preaching of Jonathan Edwards (1703–1758) took place in Northampton, Massachusetts. Edwards was not a revivalist in the usual sense of the word, but he has well been called the father of evangelical Protestantism in America. Revivals almost certainly would have occurred without him, but he became the primary apologist for, and defender of appropriate revival methods as legitimate tools of the church in performing its task. Edwards was a typical Calvinist, but in the application of his doctrinally oriented sermons, he seemed to make individualistic application to members of his congregations, with amazing results.

In the fall of 1734 and lasting into the spring of 1735, revival excitement gripped Edwards' Northampton church, and more than three hundred people were converted. The church could not hold the crowds who came to participate in the reception of all the new members. Edwards was besieged by numerous agonized citizens seeking his help in finding relief for their conviction of sin. He managed to talk individually and privately to them and thus held to a minimum any untoward public behavior that might have discredited organized religion.

As a result of this experience, in 1737 Edwards published a small work with a large title, A *Faithful Narrative of the Surprising Work of God in the Conversion of Many Hundred Souls in Northampton, and the Neighboring Towns and Villages.* The publication marked the beginning of a continuing debate with anti-enthusiasm clergymen of New England, and the controversy continued through written and spoken discourse for the remaining years of Edwards' life. Notable among opposers of the revival was Charles Chauncy (1705–1787), the prominent liberal minister of First Church in Boston.

Shortly after Edwards' experience at Northampton, George Whitefield (1714–1770), an itinerant Anglican evangelist from England, came to the colonies for his first tour, from August 1739 to January 1741. He was immediately accepted by the log-college preachers in the central colonies and quickly entered into the harvest of converts in the ongoing revival there. Dramatic results attended his first appearance, and while there was certainly opposition from the anti-revivalists, he won the support of many educated and sober-minded people—including Benjamin Franklin. Whitefield spent one month of his first tour in New England and with the help of Jonathan Edwards' literary efforts, he established a pattern of congregational revivalism that was used for the next several years. An impassioned dramatist, Whitefield preached extemporaneously, moving freely about the pulpit, never using the manuscript—a characteristic of other Calvinists of the day. He acted out human-interest stories and gave colonial America a real demonstration of drama in the pulpit.

Whitefield spent almost ten years in America, and in seven different trips, traveled from one end of the colonies to the other. During evangelizing tours he preached an average of forty hours a week. Though an Anglican, he was thoroughly catholic in outlook, and while he remained Calvinistic, his urgent persuasion to decision had inherent Arminian ideas.

The foes of revivalism were excited to strong opposition by the dramatic results of Whitefield's preaching. Then, as now, revivalism was a divisive force in the American church. Presbyterians split into the New Side and the Old Side. The Congregational revivalists had their supporters and their critics. The controversy really exploded in

1740, when Gilbert Tennent preached his famous sermon "The Danger of an Unconverted Ministry" in a revival meeting at Nottingham, on the Maryland-Pennsylvania border. Opposition to the revival had closed meeting houses in the area against the revivalists, and Tennent's congregation for this occasion was drawn largely from churches of ministers who had denied him use of their pulpits. In the sermon Tennent was inspired to strenuous objection and spoke of the resistors as ones who "hinder rather than help others in at the straight gate." He likened them to "caterpillars who labor to devour every green thing" and called on his audience to attend churches where they could benefit most. He denounced men who entered the ministry as a trade, "being unconverted themselves, with no concern for the conversion of others." His message was published and widely circulated, serving to drive the wedge even deeper in the division of Presbyterians.[4]

Gilbert Tennent disturbed the New England brethren, following Whitefield's successful tour there. Tennent had been invited to carry on Whitefield's work, but apparently his unsophisticated dress and manner, his hellfire and damnation theme, and his roaring and stomping in the pulpit aroused sharp criticism. Even so, the results of his tour of New England exceeded those of Whitefield.

John Davenport (1716–1757), a rather strange and unstable man, was unquestionably the most bizarre of the itinerant evangelists of the Great Awakening and did much to bring it into disrepute. A graduate of Yale (in 1732, at age sixteen) and a grandson of John Davenport, New Haven's founder, he was licensed to preach in 1735 and first labored on Long Island. He was strongly influenced by George Whitefield in 1740 and began to imitate Whitefield's itineracy. He arrived in Stonington, Connecticut, in 1741 and at Boston, about a year later. He was preceded into a town by his armor bearers, who marched, singing, through the streets. His view of religion was that divine revelation comes through the emotions, and he interpreted any intense feeling or thought as revelation. He began to stress total surrender to the Holy Spirit and increasingly depended on spontaneous revelation for the content of his sermons, thus causing them to lose any semblance of order or balance. Once he preached to a group for twenty-four consecutive hours, and at another point in his revivalistic activity, he burned books, wigs, cloaks, rings, and other "vanities." Small wonder that he came to represent the worst in the Awakening preaching.

As noted, the Great Awakening revival began in the middle colonies, continued there, expanded to New England, and then spread out through the southern colonies. The renewal in the South was somewhat different from that in other parts of the colonies, since it was not so much a revival as an immense missionary enterprise. There it took on more of a catholic character, without nearly the same attention to denominationalism. It was affected by the frontier nature of the southern colonies and was a prototype of the Second Great Awakening, which would occur in western Kentucky and Tennessee two generations later. The southern area was nominally Episcopalian by law, but its ministry had been notably unimpressive; the Awakening gave considerable impetus to the growth of Baptist and Methodist congregations.

As far as records can be found to explain the development of the Great Awakening in the South, it seems that one William Robinson, a former log-college student from Neshaminy, was sent (1742–1743) by the New Brunswick (New Side) Presbytery to the Virginia area. There he found an unusual revival in progress under the leadership of laymen in Hanover County. His visit and his preaching soon started a movement of revivalism that marked the beginning of a new type of Presbyterianism in the South. Following him were other log-college Presbyterian ministers: John Samuel Blair, John Roan, Samuel Finley, and William and Gilbert Tennent.

Samuel Davies (1723–1761) went in 1748 to settle among the revived Presbyterian congregation in Hanover and to serve as their pastor. For the next eleven years his name was the center of the story of revivalistic Presbyterianism in Virginia and North Carolina.

Unfortunately, space does not permit a treatment of the growth of the regular and separate Baptists and Methodists from this point. Let it be noted that the major beginnings of those organizations in America had strong impetus from the spiritual awakening generated by log-college preachers who traced their heritage back to William Tennent and Neshaminy.

The Great Awakening provided stimulation for the growth of newer denominations, in part since it provided for a new system for ministry adaptable to the frontier situation. Direct address and extemporaneous preaching were widely used in the period and led ministers to consider this mode of delivery for other pulpit occasions. The Awakening provided a challenge for the absolutism of Calvinism and encouraged the perception of a human as an individual—an individual of choice and dignity—the sort of being who increasingly would look for freedom in government, as well as freedom in religion.

THE AMERICAN REVOLUTION

The Revolutionary period of American history was an active time for churches and pulpits, though not, apparently, a time of majestic preaching by pulpit giants. Essentially every religious group had its Tories and its Patriots, along with members who were disinterested or simply apathetic about the colonial cause. The Church of England had long been identified with the British government, so Anglican clergymen were generally Tory, even though the Anglican laity in the South gave very strong support to the struggle for independence.

Among the churches, strongest support for the Revolution came from Congregational, Presbyterian, and Baptist groups. The pacifists—Quakers, Mennonites, Moravians, and Dunkards—declined to participate in the strife. The Dutch and German Reformed churches and the Lutheran churches with no particular heritage for or against the British, generally favored the colonies. Catholics and Jews, both groups very few in number, were most often supportive of the colonial cause.

Peter Oliver, an arch Tory, wrote in 1781 that if one wished to understand the rage for patriotism that swept the colonies into war, one should look to "Mr. Otis's black regiment, the dissenting clergy."[5] As suggested previously, the clergymen of that day commanded unusual attention and respect from the church and from the public. Their education placed them among the most competent men of the community, and the nature of their office and interests presented an unassailable goodwill toward their audiences. Robert Friedenberg has examined the place of the clergy in the Revolutionary cause. He makes an interesting comparison between a sermon of Jonathan Mayhew (1720–1766), minister of West

Church in Boston, known for his liberalism and his defense of liberal theories of government, and John Locke's two treatises on government, which were probably the most widely cited statements of political philosophy used by colonials in the Revolutionary period. He concludes that the religious justification for rebellion as evidenced by Mayhew's sermon, and the secular justification as evidenced by Locke's writing, are virtually identical, save for their conclusions concerning the origin of human rights. Mayhew maintained that the authority of government derives from God; Locke felt that all men are naturally in a state of nature and will remain so until they voluntarily make themselves members of some politic society. Thus for Mayhew and the colonial clergy, the source of government authority was God; for Locke and most of the secular leaders of the time, the source of government authority was the contractual consent of the governed.

So both Mayhew and secular leaders determined that government should function for the good of the people. Thus when the people decide that government is not operating for their good, they have every right to change it. Rebellion is thereby justified. To the extent that the colonial ministry articulated these principles, they positively influenced the movement for independence. They spoke to large audiences, many of whom were unlikely to be reached by any other means. So it was that in 1776, with the counsel and encouragement of numbers of their clergymen, American colonials declared their independence, confidently acting "with the firm reliance on the protection of divine providence."[6]

The inevitable war for independence followed close on the signing of the Declaration of Independence, and much to the surprise of both sides and numerous interested foreign powers, the tattered army of the colonists eventually won the contest. It only remained, then, to discard the outmoded Articles of Confederation and to design a comprehensive and lasting frame of government. That action took place in Philadelphia during the late spring and summer of 1787, when our present Constitution was hammered out by fifty-five wise and far-sighted men from the thirteen federated states. The people were then ready to get on with the business of building a nation and establishing a culture. In this effort the churches and their ministers were destined to play a major role.

The Church of England in America was the greatest ecclesiastical casualty of the Revolution. It was stripped of its privileges, prestige, and support, and its congregations were depleted by defections to Methodism, which developed into an autonomous denomination following the war. Congregationalists, Presbyterians, and Baptists, the three other denominations of British heritage, tied together by common acceptance of the Westminster Confession, were the largest American denominations. All had been strongly identified with the colonial cause and survived the war with increased prestige. They added considerable strength to the moral struggles of the expanding frontier.

Soon after the war there were some seven hundred Congregational churches, most led by native American-trained ministers; and about six hundred Presbyterian congregations with finely trained ministers, mostly American. Baptists had ranked considerably behind the other two groups prior to the war, but soon experienced such rapid growth that by 1800, ministering primarily to the common people, they had grown to be the largest American denomination. Their preacher-farmer ministry, the extreme flexibility of their ecclesiastical structure, the ease with which they communicated with the ordinary folk on the frontier—all contributed to their accelerated growth.

Other organized religious groups present in the new nation included Episcopalians (former Anglicans) who were fourth in actual number at the time, although quite unpopular and viewed with some suspicion; 95 Quaker meetings; 250 Dutch and German Reformed congregations; 200 Lutheran churches; 50 Roman Catholic churches; 37 Methodist circuits; and some 60 German sects.[7]

At the time of the war, Roman Catholics numbered some twenty-five thousand, most of that number landed gentry, concentrated primarily in Pennsylvania and Maryland, the only two colonies without prejudicial statutes against Catholics. After the war, Roman Catholicism also experienced rapid expansion, accompanied by intense growing pains. Tension developed between the older population, who were migrants from Ireland and southern Germany, and the many new arrivals from the French settlements along the Mississippi, which now became American territory. Priests from abroad, usually French, did not serve well as pastors of Irish or German congregations, and so as early as 1791, the French Sulpicians transformed One Mile Tavern, just beyond Baltimore, into St. Mary's Seminary, to provide training for a native priesthood. It remained the primary seminary for the American Catholic Church for nearly two decades. Catholics continued to have major internal problems until well into the twentieth century.

After the Revolution, migrations beyond the Alleghenies to the Mississippi River prompted an intense struggle between civilized Christian morality and the barbaric social practices endemic to the individualism of the frontier. The very nature of the future character of the nation hung in the balance of that struggle. It was in that period and on that front that the Second Great Awakening in western Kentucky and western Tennessee occurred and helped to turn the tide in favor of a relatively civilized society.

THE EARLY NATIONAL PERIOD

The new "Americans" opted for religious freedom as articulated in the Bill of Rights in 1791, and this put all church groups on an equal footing; each could rise or fall, prosper or fail, according to its own persuasive abilities. The government would no longer recognize a state church or levy taxes for its support. All colonial laws penalizing Catholics were removed, and freedom of worship was established for all Protestants (however, it was as late as 1833 before Massachusetts revoked its state-church privilege). Religious liberty had come, persuasion was now the order of the day, and the churches—all of them—faced both their greatest opportunity and their greatest threat.

Westward movement, building of new communities, forming of new territories, and the admission of new states into the union occupied the two generations following independence. While the churches were engaged in significant dialogue on theological issues in the East, important work was being performed, as ministers and church groups attempted to serve the religious needs of the ever-expanding restless western frontier.

Prior to the Revolution there had been small settlements south of the Ohio River. But soon afterward there was a virtual stampede of optimistic, courageous, free and equal, and usually young, men and women moving westward to look for economic opportunities. They pulled up stakes, cut family ties, loaded their possessions, and headed west, leaving their churches, and often their religion, behind.

The institutional church faced various degrees of difficulty in pursuing and ministering to these people. Thus it was that the task of following the population west fell to the churches with a flexible ecclesiastical structure and a religious concern for the class of migrating people. Generally, these were the Baptists, the Methodists, and to a limited extent, the Presbyterians—the three American churches that made the greatest impact on the early generations of the American frontier.

The frontier Baptist minister typically was a farmer-preacher, who labored with his hands during the week and with his Bible and voice on Sunday. He usually had not been sent by any church or missionary society. The Presbyterian frontier minister typically was a school teacher, supported by a church or presbytery—a man with sound education and theological training, but still not a full-time minister. The Methodist circuit rider, on the other hand, gave full time to his religious duties, preaching daily on a circuit that might be three to four hundred miles long.

One notable phase of frontier religion was the development of the camp meeting as a unique way of adjusting to the religious needs of a shifting population. The idea was introduced in Logan County, Kentucky, in 1797, by James McGready (1758?–1817), a Presbyterian minister. The concept of using the camp meeting as an annual religious rally spread quickly over the frontier from western Kentucky into Tennessee, and ultimately throughout the frontier north of the Ohio, as well as further on into the Deep South.

The greatest number of people ever assembled in a frontier camp meeting was at Cane Ridge in Bourbon County, Kentucky, on August 6, 1801. The crowd was estimated at between ten and twenty-five thousand, and that was at a time when the state's largest city, nearby Lexington, had a population of about two thousand. The meeting was under Presbyterian management and was called by Presbyterian minister Barton Warren Stone (1772–1844), who was serving the Cane Ridge Church. People and ministers of all denominations came, however, as well as thousands who had no religious affiliation at all.

At the Cane Ridge meeting, striking events took place. Six or seven evangelists addressed the crowds at the same time from different points. Great numbers of the listeners fell to the ground, while others "got the jerks" amid general noise and confusion. When the meeting was over, after almost a week, Cane Ridge was referred to as the greatest outpouring of the Spirit since Pentecost. It was a watershed in American church history.[8]

Some Presbyterians, accustomed to quietness, dignity, and a rational approach to religion, found the results of the meeting distasteful. Other Presbyterians supported it, and they promptly divided on the issue of revivalism, as had Presbyterians in the 1740s. Those favoring revivalism later became the Cumberland Presbyterians.

From this time there developed two distinct types of revivalism— the Presbyterian-Congregational-Calvinistic rational type, depending heavily on listeners who had been well grounded in the basic teaching of the church prior to the revival; and the Methodist-Baptist-Disciple type, less restricted and appealing to the religiously illiterate. Even with the differing emphases, camp-meeting revivals prospered, so that in 1811 there were more than four hundred, and by 1820 there were nearly a thousand camp meetings annually.

The growth and flourishing of the camp meeting on the frontier roughly parallels a period of general religious revival throughout the colonies. During the 1790s, scattered revivals had occurred among the Congregationalists in remote sections of New England. A notable revival among students at Hampden-Sydney and Washington colleges in 1787 produced some forty Presbyterian ministers. In central and western New York there were so many revivals in 1800 that it was noted as the "year of the great revival." In 1802, Timothy Dwight (1752–1817), president of Yale and a grandson of Jonathan Edwards, preached a series of chapel addresses resulting in an unintended revival, at which one-third of the student body of Yale was converted.

Graduates of John McMillan's log college in Washington, Pennsylvania, among them James McGready of camp meeting note, had spread out into the Carolinas, Kentucky, and Tennessee and were largely responsible for the quickening religious interests of that area at the beginning of the nineteenth century.

The revivals of this period were similar to the revivals of the First Great Awakening, expect that the ministers of the Second Awakening sought to promote the revival by using *means* to evoke decisions from the hearers. Earlier revivalists apparently had not consciously used such techniques.

Charles Grandison Finney (1792–1875) easily could be pointed to as the most successful evangelist of the nineteenth century. He had been a lawyer in Adams, New York, was active in the church, studied for the ministry after a conversion experience, and became a most effective preacher. His presentations were simple and yet highly structured, revealing his legal training. He spoke directly, bluntly, and without mannerism, so that his audience could not misunderstand him. He said that he merely talked about things that other ministers preached about. Western New York literally caught fire in response to his plain proclamation of the Christian gospel. Finney went on to head Oberlin College in Ohio, where he trained other evangelists in his methods. He epitomizes the work of the Second Great Awakening among American Protestant churches—a work that was carried on by scores of Lutherans, Dutch Reformed, Congregationalists, Baptists, Methodists, and a growing number of preachers in the restoration movement, then called Christians or Disciples.

In tracing preaching in the early national period, much stress has been placed on revivals and camp meetings as opposed to organized churches and their pastors. It should be noted that the meetings and revivals were sponsored by pastors and churches and that converts did not automatically become members of a given church. Each church had its own procedures for the admission of new members and it was necessary that converts be approached and persuaded to join a specific group.

On the frontier, interdenominational relations were frequently unpleasant. There were skirmishes: Protestants against Protestants; denominations against sects; Protestants against Catholics. The Baptists, Methodists, and Presbyterians usually gained an early foothold in a new area and competed vigorously for the citizens of their parish. Often an intruding new group became a common enemy. Considerable pulpit time was consumed in seeking to delineate the differences between Baptists and Methodists, Baptists and Presbyterians, Presbyterians and Disciples, or Congregationalists and Presbyterians. The Roman Catholic clergy, still attempting to assimilate Catholic immigrants from differing cultures, generally moved onto the frontier *with* their people rather than moving into an area and attempting to missionize. Wherever a small group of Catholics did assemble as a parish, Protestant churches often pulled themselves together into a semblance of opposing unity.

This competition between denominations, with its resulting dissipation of energies, was one of the motivations for the American revival of an issue that had had recurring emphasis throughout Christian history—the unity of the Christian church. The restoration issue, or the attempt to restore pristine New Testament Christianity based on the simple, clear teaching of the Bible, surfaced during this period under the leadership of Barton Stone, of Cane Ridge fame, and Alexander Campbell (1788–1866), an itinerant preacher. The hope was that all Christians could unify under simple New Testament principles. The Disciples of Christ, the Christian Church, and the Churches of Christ all look to the restoration movement as significant in their heritage, if not actually in their origin.

In the East, a general, well-coordinated revolt against prevailing doctrinal orthodoxy led to an acceptance of Unitarianism, Universalism, and Deism among some ministers and congregations. In reality, the doctrine of the Trinity was not the primary matter of contention; the issue was God's sovereignty versus the individual's freedom. The principal documents on the liberal side of the issue were William Ellery Channing's Baltimore sermon at the ordination of Jared Sparks; Ralph Waldo Emerson's divinity school address; and Theodore Parker's South Boston sermon. Each address manifested an increasing "man-centeredness" and ultimately resulted in the founding of the American Unitarian Association. Of the sixteen pre-Revolutionary Congregational churches in Boston, fourteen were tending toward Unitarianism in the first decade of the nineteenth century. The movement continued to spread into smaller towns of the vicinity. In 1805, Henry Ware, an avowed Unitarian, was elected to the Hollis Professorship of Theology at Harvard. This marked the beginning of a trend that resulted in the founding of rigorously orthodox Andover Theological Seminary in 1808.

The establishment of Andover presented a shift toward formal, standard, professional ministerial training, following a three-year curriculum. Earlier schools of divinity or departments of religion had enrolled a limited number of ministerial candidates at a time, and they had attended classes in a noninsulated environment amid other students of the arts and sciences. In contrast, by 1820 Andover had well over one hundred students studying in a cloistered setting, apart from daily interaction with students of "profane and common" disciplines. Thus began the practice of isolating theological education in American Protestantism. Young men, and at a later date young women, were gathered into an institution designed solely and exclusively for professional training of the clergy. They were removed from the seats of secular learning where they might have continued to hear about literature, economics, science, politics, and the like, as well as theology; where they might have shared classes and dialogue with typical future congregants. Instead, moved into a sacred, insulated, seminary setting, theological students tended to develop thought-patterns and professional vocabularies well removed from real life, where theology must have its greatest impact. The cloistering of theological education in America among Protestants has had a very negative impact on the communication of the gospel and the work of the church. Roman Catholics, with centuries of cloistered theological education, have experienced similar difficulties in trying to talk simply and intelligibly about the gospel to their people.

Meanwhile, increased immigration of Catholics to the now united colonies led to the formation of missionary societies among European Catholics to help their coreligionists in the New World. The Jesuits, revived in 1805 after having been papally suppressed in 1773, were of considerable aid to American Roman Catholicism in seeking to organize the church in America. By 1835, every large city in the United States contained religious houses of Ursulines, Carmelites, the Sacred Heart, or the order of Sisters of Charity. Dioceses were established in Charleston, Richmond, Cincinnati, Mobile, St. Louis, Detroit, Vincennes, Dubuque, Little Rock, Nashville, Natchez, Pittsburgh, Milwaukee, Chicago, Hartford,

Oregon City, Albany, Buffalo, Cleveland, and Galveston, so that by 1850 practically every city of any size in the country had become the site of a diocesan headquarters.

Bishop John England (1786–1842) of Charleston and Bishop John Hughes (1797–1864) of New York were two outstanding Catholic leaders of the early national period. England traveled continuously by carriage throughout a territory eight hundred miles in length and two to three hundred miles in width, preaching and administering the sacraments. Bishop Hughes, who laid the cornerstone of St. Patrick's Cathedral in New York City in 1858, was involved in helping the waves of Catholic immigrants, especially those from Ireland, as they settled in the new country. He was particularly effective in dealing with a New York public-school society issue.

Membership in the American Roman Catholic Church grew from about 600,000 in 1830 to 3.5 million in 1850 and to 4.5 million by the outbreak of the Civil War. The maintenance of a Catholic identity and their acceptance as legitimately religious people were the two main concerns at that time. They found it necessary to begin an extensive system of parochial schools, not because they were necessarily opposed to secular schools, but because the public schools of the day were strongly Protestant-oriented. And, as mentioned before, Catholic immigrants came to America from assorted places in eastern, western, northern, and southern Europe, each group with its own practices and culture. Non–English-speaking Catholics found it difficult to fit into established American parishes, a problem leading to the formation of ethnic parishes within many dioceses. This practice produced a realistic ministry, if not a cultural assimilation into "the American way."

ABOLITION AND CIVIL WAR

Both proslavery and abolitionist preachers mounted pulpits in America after 1830 to defend their positions on the basis of scripture; the sinfulness of slaveholding was the central issue. Southern preachers in the main defended slavery as a positive good, citing biblical justification for slavery and divine support for civil laws regulating slavery. Abolitionist preachers rejected the civil law on the basis of appeal to a higher law and cited scripture to condemn slavery.

Supermilitant William Lloyd Garrison (1805–1879), a preacher of sorts and an agitator superior, established his publication *The Liberator* in 1831 and called for immediate emancipation. Three years later, two young preachers who would soon be heard on the issue of slavery were classmates at Harvard Divinity School: Theodore Parker (1810–1860) and James H. Thornwell (1812–1862). Parker completed his study, adopted a strong abolitionist stance, and became one of the leaders in the antislavery pulpit in the 1840s and 1850s. Thornwell, on the other hand, dissatisfied with the liberal intellectual and theological climate of the Boston area, returned to the South, was later ordained a Presbyterian minister, and became an influential professor at South Carolina College and later at Columbia Theological Seminary. He presented his theological justification of slavery in his sermon "Rights and Duties of Masters," delivered March 26, 1850, at the dedication of a church erected for the religious instruction of Negroes in Charleston, South Carolina. The sermon was duplicated and distributed widely throughout the South.

These divergent views on the issue of slavery led to the rupture of fellowship in several Protestant denominations. Looking back, it seems quite clear that perceptions of theology were often cultural and geographical. Later, after the war began, the same cultural distortions were evident in preaching. Civil War sermons in both North and South showed a blind loyalty to the geographical origin of the speakers. Vested interests of the territory of the churches seem to have greatly affected the homiletic approaches taken; and the universal conviction seems to have been that each individual preacher and his congregation were on the right side in the struggle.

Both sides operated from the principle that God controlled the universe in all its aspects. Thus God had caused the war for his own purposes: to end or to protect slavery; to end rebellion or to insure southern independence; or to punish the nation for its sins with the understanding that neither section could win, short of full submission to the will of God. The southern cause—to preserve the independence of the South—remained the same throughout the war; the northern cause reflected changing events during the period.

Probably all speakers are to some degree guilty of operating from premises derived from culturally skewed perceptions, but such misperceptions were especially blatant in the abolition and Civil War preachers. Since preachers treat matters of supreme importance, they hold a high duty to verify both premise and perception.

THE AGE OF REFORM

When the village of Chicago was incorporated in 1833, it consisted of seventeen scattered houses along the shores of Lake Michigan; in 1900, it numbered 1.7 million residents and was the fifth largest city in the world. Its dramatic growth demonstrates major trends in American society concurrent with the rise of industrial capitalism following the Civil War. These profound changes affected the church and its preaching. The churches, of course, needed to recover from the ravages of the war and while the preachers were shaped by the new movements in society, few of them sought to address the problem of the growing maldistribution of wealth.

The rapid and radical changes in social, economic, and religious conditions immediately following the Civil War normally would have produced a setting for certain revival efforts, but the accumulation of wealth by parishioners blunted the strong evangelical emphasis in the freer churches. Large and wealthy urban churches provided creative outlets not only for preachers, but for architects, artists, musicians, and even church administrators. Notable ministers of the day included George A. Gordon (1853–1929) at Boston's Old South Church; Theodore Thornton Munger and Newman Smyth at two historical Congregational churches in New Haven; Thomas DeWitt Talmage at Central Presbyterian in New York; and Southern Baptist preacher-scholar John A. Broadus (1827–1905).

Standing half a head taller in talent and performance than a score of other pulpit giants of the day, however, were Henry Ward Beecher (1813–1887) of Plymouth Congregational Church in Brooklyn and Phillips Brooks (1835-1893) of Trinity Episcopal Church in Boston. A debate has continued for years as to which of these two men was the greatest preacher who ever lived. Neither possessed an oratorical style that would find broad acceptance today.

Henry Ward was the fourth son of Lyman Beecher, stalwart defender of the orthodox faith against Unitarianism and rationalism in the early decades of the nineteenth century. Henry preached revivalistically in small churches in Indiana until he was called to the new Plymouth Congregational Church in 1847. There he proceeded to remove all the pulpit furniture except a very narrow lectern, from which he preached extemporaneously. He read extensively on the subjects of his sermons and usually did not prepare even an outline. He often addressed topics of the time, including contemporary social and political issues: slavery, reconstruction, immigration, taxes, women's rights. He sought to accommodate Christianity with the theory of evolution and with biblical criticism. Annually, from 1872 to 1874, he delivered the Yale lectures on preaching.

Phillips Brooks was a bachelor, a gentleman, a scholar, and in addition, an orator in the pulpit. His eloquent and scholarly sermons reflected careful biblical study, a strong pastoral heart, and some insensitivity to the inequities in American life of his time. To him, the sufferings of the city were in large part deserved, but he felt they were only temporary problems, which God's purposes would certainly correct. His ministry represents, even in its marvelous success, the capitalistic captivity of the American Protestant church in the cities during the age of rising industrialism. He and others were successful in keeping a remarkable number of America's great men of business in active support of the work of the church. Sadly, though, their corporate impact prevented the church from addressing its social responsibility directly.

The rapid growth of the American cities after 1880, however, created conditions which encouraged a new thrust of revivalism. Thousands of people, moving into the cities from smaller places in the United States and from abroad, lost contact with their churches. Revivalistic campaigns designed to reach such people began about this time and flourished well into the 1920s.

Dwight L. Moody (1837–1899) began his revival efforts even before the 1880s. He had been a successful young shoe salesman, a key worker in the YMCA Sunday School movement in Chicago, and an especially effective fund raiser for the YMCA before he moved into mass evangelism in the cities. He joined forces with chorister Ira Sankey, and for twenty-two years they worked together as a revival team. In Great Britain, from 1873 to 1875, they were heard by three to four million people. Moody's message was a simple blend of optimism and freewill acceptance of the love of God. His only concern in preaching was the conversion of sinners; anything else was secondary. He believed that the social and moral conditions of the burgeoning cities needed to be changed, but that they could be changed only by reconstructed, regenerated people; converted individuals would solve all personal and social problems. He planned to do his part in helping God regenerate all for whom Jesus died. Moody retired in 1892, with no successor of equal status. He was followed, however, by scores of other successful preacher/evangelists, including J. Wilbur Chapman, Reuben A. Torrey, Samuel Porter Jones, Benjamin Fay Mills, and finally Billy Sunday, who joined singer Homer A. Rodeheaver to form a team resembling that of Moody and Sankey.

William Ashley Sunday (1863–1935) was an Iowa farm boy who gained some prominence as a professional baseball player for the Chicago White Sox. He was converted after moving to Chicago and began to work in the YMCA. Ultimately he helped to organize revival campaigns with J. Wilbur Chapman, and when Chapman took a Philadelphia pastorate, he named Sunday his campaign successor. Billy moved slowly from a start in Garner, Iowa, in 1895, into the revival circuits of the larger cities. By 1917 he drew almost 1.5 million listeners to a ten-week campaign in New York; converts of the meeting were numbered at 98,264.

Billy Sunday's success has been attributed to his ability to dramatize, using bodily contortions—sliding into a pulpit "home plate," breaking up pulpit furniture—and to an unceasing torrent of words. His crude but graphic word choices inflamed the elite and charmed the common. To him the most moderate of social drinkers was a "dirty, low-down, whiskey-soaked, beer guzzling, bull-necked, foul-mouthed hypocrite." He defined sin in terms of individual moralism, based on values that he himself defined. The altar call climaxed each of his services, and public decision was made easy; the sawdust trail was wide and all downhill, as Billy pleaded, "Do you want God's blessings on you, your home, your church, your nation? . . . If you do, raise your hands." Then he went on at times to ask, "How many of you men and women will jump to your feet and come on down and say 'Bill, here's my hand for God, for home, for my native land, to live and conquer for Christ'?"[9] Usually one in ten responded to that call as Homer and the choir began their musical background for the walk to the front.

Mass evangelism among American Protestants reached its peak immediately prior to World War I when there were at least 650 active evangelists and some 1,200 part-timers in the United States. But the war came and the number of converts of the evangelistic campaign trail inevitably diminished. After World War I, America's religious climate changed radically, and evangelistic campaigns declined. Now, except perhaps for the work of Southern Baptists, the revival has all but disappeared along the large evangelical churches.

Meanwhile American Roman Catholics were coping with problems associated with an influx of more than 5 million people in some thirty years. These masses were working toward acceptance in a basically Protestant country at the same time they were attempting to bring some sort of order into their church life. Prior to the 1880s, most of the Catholic immigrants had settled in rural areas, with the exception of the Irish, who had little money to move inland and stayed in the Eastern Seaboard cities. After 1880 the surge of immigrants included Czechs, Slovaks, Poles, Russians, Ukranians, Hungarians, Bulgarians, Lithuanians, Latvians, Greeks, Armenians, Portuguese, Italians, and Mexicans, from both the Latin and the Byzantine rites. Those of the Byzantine or Armenian rite were sometimes led by married clergy, and all too often were treated as heretical groups by normative Latin-rite clergy. For a time, Latin-rite Catholics could receive instruction in their native language until they learned English; for Eastern-rite Catholics, the language barrier was compounded by the differing-rite problem. This situation was finally addressed directly with the formation of separate dioceses for Byzantine-rite Catholics.

It was an almost insurmountable task to minister to these millions of people with all their Old World cultural differences and their thirty or more languages. The situation was not faced without some abuse. It was a problem not unlike the one faced by Methodists, Baptists, and Presbyterians on the early frontier; both involved uprooted peoples of vastly divergent cultures. The Catholic assimilation situation was not helped by the fact that most of the new millions emerged from the lower economic and cultural strata of Europe. Needless to say, the clergy were faced less with problems of homiletic excellence than with the responsibility for educating and organizing their parishes. A happy note for their task, however, was the nature of Catholic worship in relation to the concepts of the faith. Much of the content of the faith had been ritualized through centuries of visual and nonverbal usage. This act minimized total dependence on language, but even that dependence could rely on Latin as something of a common language for most of the people.

Unhappily it would be decades before the fundamental assimilation problem of American Catholicism would be solved and attention could be turned to a noble and persuasive pulpit. The acceptance of Fulton J. Sheen and John F. Kennedy in our era typifies the acceptance of their religion in the United States, and now the American public may expect to hear much more from that body of Christians from which came Augustine, Francis, Savonarola, and Wycliffe. And we can be sure that, despite the hardship of adjustment, many Americn cities would have been far more depraved, had it not been for the leveling influence of the Catholic church.

One other element of the American scene that requires examination at this point is the development of the black Protestant church during and after the Reconstruction period. Prior to emancipation there were few independent Negro churches except in the North, where the African Methodist Episcopal Church and some Baptist churches had been organized in the second decade of the nineteenth century. Before the Civil War, blacks generally had worshiped with whites, being assigned to the back seats or the galleries of the churches. Slave owners, contrary to what might have been said, most often recognized their responsibility to teach their slaves duties to God as well as to man. After emancipation, blacks were not forced to leave the white churches, but most did leave as a matter of choice.

Many free, educated blacks from the North moved to the South following the Civil War to find positions of leadership in the communities and in the churches. Both northern and southern white churches assisted blacks in building churches, schools, and colleges and in securing a trained and ordained ministry. The northern churches often viewed the South as a mission field and developed missionary and educational agencies to work among blacks. Today a number of excellent schools and colleges graduate well-trained black leaders of whom any culture could be proud.

Typically, black religion of the post-Civil War period reflected generations of slavery, and preaching generally dwelt on other-worldly biblical images and concepts. Death, release, and the blessings of heaven were recurring themes. Much black preaching still is concerned with these topics.

Legal limits were placed on their full participation in civic, political, and economic life, so blacks viewed the church as the one institution that they fully controlled. In the church they could attain places of leadership and opportunities to express themselves. Probably this accounts for the very high pecentage of black church members who are Baptists and Methodists, since there is great opportunity for lay leadership and self-expression in those organizations.

While the church provided blacks a badly needed refuge in a hostile world, it also has provided some impetus for economic cooperation in business and housing. It has published influential periodicals and aided black education. The black church has served as a vital means of preserving a sense of racial solidarity, but possibly its greatest flaw has been its submissive lack of concern for temporal black existence in a world of white supremacy. The quest for personal dignity in society for black people had to wait, with rare exceptions, until the coming of the black revolution in the 1950s and the development of black theology in the 1970s.

IV. PREACHING:
TWENTIETH-CENTURY AMERICA

AN OVERVIEW

The newly developed internal combustion engine and the oil boom ushered in the twentieth century with its emphasis on production and consumer goods. These developments presaged much of what was to follow in the next eight decades as our society moved faster and faster in an effort to own and consume more and more.

Among the notable occurrences in the church about which preaching has centered, have been the peaking, plateauing, and falling away of the missionary emphasis; the rise and fall of the social-gospel movement and the internalization of it in many church groups; the increase and continuation of ecumenical trends; the post-World War II religious revival in essentially all of American Christendom; the maturation of the black church; the acceptance of Catholicism into mainstream American life; the ecclesiastical implications of the women's movement; the development of the "electric church"; the growth of Pentecostalism; and the widespread emergence of cults in answer to the demand for instant salvation.

Several of the topics in this chapter relate to the issues of society in general. Preaching has always adjusted to and been affected by social factors, but we will report more about such matters in the twentieth century because, obviously, we are closer to them, we know more about them, and because the interaction of church and societal issues is particularly prominent in this period.

FOREIGN MISSIONS CHANGE

John R. Mott (1865–1955), leading American ambassador of missions and ecumenism for almost a half century, was rallying the Christian missionary forces at the turn of the twentieth century for a final campaign to "win the world for Christ in a single generation." He was not alone in his optimism about an America caught up in social Darwinism and the deluding concept that social and human progress, including progressive revelation about God, were inevitable. For almost a century before World War I, the American Protestant missionary effort prospered, and William Warren Sweet pointed out that,

> from the close of the Spanish-American War, American Christian people were becoming increasingly internationally-minded. In the Protestant churches generally the foreign missionary interest was the dominant interest . . . and there were few sincere Christian young men and women in the colleges during those years who did not consider the question of giving themselves to some type of foreign Christian service.[1]

But along with their message of Christianity, many of our foreign missionaries were exporting a heavy dose of American culture.

> At their mission posts they lived in Western-style compounds where the natives never entered the front door but slippered around to the back door to do the hard labor for a handful of coins. Naked little girls were decently covered in pinafores and little boys with drawers. All were taught to sing "Jesus Loves Me"—in English, of course, since this was the foreordained language of salvation.[2]

The great day of the Lord seemed to be at hand when Christian democracy would rule the nation and the world. Thus, when the United States finally entered the Great War in 1917, it was interpreted, by some Protestants at least, as a virtuous effort to save Christian civilization; it was essentially a Holy War. Church leaders could not foresee the radical decline in optimism and idealism that would follow the war and the lost peace.

General disillusionment set in, and Protestant missions were greatly affected. The 1920s were a time of extraordinary reaction against idealism and reform, and one manifestation was a declining interest in missions and missionary giving. There was the added factor that the "heathen" did not welcome us as heartily as in the past and in some cases actually resisted our westernizing religious efforts. "The hallelujah faith sank under the weight of the secular image it carried of Western culture and conquest."[3] By the time the Foreign Missions Conference of North America met in 1926, missionary leaders were dismayed at the attitude of local churches toward the cause of missions, the decline in the missionary force, and the waning interest of young people in responding to the missionary challenge. In 1920, there were 2,700 students who volunteered for mission service; in 1928, only 252.[4]

But the wise old bishops and the mission board chairpeople learned important lessons, in examining the plight of their programs. They swept out all patronizing, cultivated airs of superiority over natives, and now our missionaries go out carrying no image but the cross and with only enough baggage to avoid culture shock. The missionaries have learned that they must preach a gospel—a kerygma—cut free of any cultural bias of their own. Evangelized persons, of whatever culture, will make their own peculiar cultic expressions of the Christian faith.

THE SOCIAL GOSPEL

The social-gospel emphasis, from approximately 1875 to 1915, was the church's response to social and economic inequities growing out of industrial capitalism and the accumulation of great fortunes. Baptist Walter Rauschenbusch (1861–1918), Congregationalist George Herron (1862–1925), Congregationalist Washington Gladden (1836–1918), and numerous other ministers worked through the churches and from their pulpits to bring about social reform and to establish God's kingdom on earth—a kind of society that would infuse Christian concern and a love-thy-neighbor attitude into the business and labor world. Leaders of the movement were preachers, counselors, and educators, rather than activists. They were preachers, not "doers," of the social gospel. Their work had its roots in the Age of Reason, in the growing emphasis on the place of man in theology, and in the general belief that reforming society would make men and women better beings.

The social gospel solidified into a movement when evangelicals of the late nineteenth century split into liberal and conservative forces; liberals turned to social issues, while conservatives were concerned primarily with private issues. This split became institutionalized in 1908 with the formation of the Federal Council of Churches, which consolidated the social endeavors of the liberal churches. The conservatives counterorganized and began to shape the fundamentalist movement.

The fundamentalist-modernist controversy developed from this division and was prominent in the period between 1918 and 1930. Baptist Harry Emerson Fosdick (1878–1969), serving as associate minister of preaching at First Presbyterian Church in New York City, was primary leader and spokesman for the amorphous modernist movement. The more vocal fundamentalists had several defenders. Clarence E. Macartney (1879–1957) of Arch Street Presbyterian Church in Philadelphia was the most articulate of the conservatives, but William Bell Riley and William Jennings Bryan (1860–1925) spoke more often and widely. Both of the latter injected the issue of evolution into the controversy, in addition to the *sine qua non* five points of fundamentalism: the infallibility of the Bible, Christ's virgin birth, his substitutionary atonement, his resurrection, and his second coming. The issue of evolution, much discussed in state legislatures, came to a climax in the "Scopes monkey trial" in Dayton, Tennessee, in 1925.

Much of the social-gospel controversy was literary. Among Protestants, the modernist-fundamentalist debate, as a spin-off of the social-gospel emphasis, was argued primarily in the pulpit. The issue in Roman Catholicism, however, was handled largely by documentary exchange in the hierarchy.

The social gospel tended to be popular or revolutionary, depending to a great extent upon the socioeconomic status of the group to which it was addressed. Never very popular with the economically comfortable, it was more palatable to the afflicted of society. In 1928 Reinhold Niebuhr (1892-1970) joined the faculty of Union Theological Seminary in New York City, where he became an effective critic and prolific writer of books stressing a modern version of Calvinism and a most penetrating critique of optimistic liberalism. The social gospel fought but failed to survive the neo-Calvinism/neo-orthodoxy Niebuhr preached, and presently it left the pulpit from which it had sought to afflict the comfortable. Churches, like people who are criticized, first tend to make repeated denials of guilt, but after consideration, most take criticism to heart and often change their behavior. And so in spite of the demise of the movement as such, the social gospel has become an integral part of the thought and action of large sections of the Christian church. Personified in Martin Luther King, Jr., the social gospel won the Nobel Peace Prize in 1964, as King sought to love his enemies into responsible action toward his black brothers; and again in 1979, in the person of Mother Teresa, the saint of the gutters of Calcutta. The social gospel lives wherever people, in the name of Christ, feed the hungry, give drink to the thirsty, clothe the naked, visit the sick, or go to those in prison.

THE ECUMENICAL MOVEMENT

For much of church history, Christians have shown a desire to present a unified front to the world. A recurring effort in that direction has been the drive for all Christians to return to pristine New Testament Christianity as the ideal unifying life-style. During the early and middle parts of the nineteenth century, Thomas and Alexander Campbell joined this refrain and were quite effective in their efforts to restore simple, primitive, New Testament church life in Kentucky, Ohio, and Tennessee. The ecumenical movement as we now know it, however, was an outgrowth of the missionary activity of the latter part of the nineteenth century. It had its origin when overseas missionaries found it impossible to make denqmina-tionalism a real issue for new converts from non-Christian religions. Additionally, the widespread advance of world missions required careful allocation of resources and some interdenominational agency to serve as a clearing house of information. These concerns, which seemed to recommend cooperation in missionary activities at home and abroad, led to the establishment of several councils and agencies. The Federal Council of the Churches of Christ in America was established in 1908 by some thirty Protestant denominations. The World Missionary Conference followed shortly in Edinburgh in 1910. World War I intervened, but then in 1927, the World Conference on Faith and Order met at Lausanne, and a decade later the Conference on Church, Community, and State was held at Oxford, England. These three movements—missionary, life and work, and faith and order—led to the founding of the World Council of Churches on August 22, 1948, with representatives from 146 churches in forty-four countries. Shortly afterward in 1950, came the founding of the National Council of Churches of Christ in the United States as an interdenominational body representing twenty-nine churches. It replaced the Federal Council of Churches and seven other interdenominational agencies. This occasioned much sectarian, and even inflammatory, pulpit rhetoric, but not much of it was directed specifically toward the topic of church unity itself.

Communication on the ecumenical movement has been largely that of conference, assembly, pamphlet, position paper, and book, rather than that of preaching, except in rare circumstances. On selected pulpit occasions, Protestant denominational leaders have addressed sermons to the issue of Christian unity. Such was the case when Eugene Carson Blake, general secretary of the World Council of Churches and stated clerk of the General Assembly of the Presbyterian Church U.S.A., was invited by Bishop James Pike to preach in Grace Cathedral, San Francisco, on December 4, 1960. Audaciously, he proposed the joining of the Protestant Episcopal Church, the Presbyterian Church U.S.A., the United Church of Christ, and the Methodist Church, to form a plan of church union both catholic and reformed. This proposal ultimately led to COCU, the Consultation on Church Union, which has had only moderate success in uniting the four bodies. Dr. Blake spelled out some fundamental criteria for church union which could be used as a basis for dialogue toward reuniting the church.

Some significant church bodies, notably Southern Baptists, essentially ignored the ecumenical movement, while some ultraconservatives fulminated against it. One significant conservative was the analytical and articulate Carl F. H. Henry, theologian, writer, and founding editor of *Christianity Today*. A careful statement opposing organic union of the Christian church is found in his sermon "Christ and His Embattled Legions," in which he stressed the present spiritual unity of all Christians but affirmed that organic union will not be a reality until the Second Coming of Christ.[5]

The Christian church has not progressed as rapidly in organic union as ecumenical leaders, particularly those involved in the National Council of Churches, have desired. "We have lived through a winter of ecumenism, but the spring is coming," said Dr. Paul Crow in a major 1978 report on the state of the ecumenical movement. "Unity belongs to the essence of the church . . . [but] casual ecumenism and token cooperation are the rites which the churches compose for their life-styles."[6]

The cultural disruption of the 1960s and the resulting decline in membership of the churches threatened the jobs of some pastors and denominational leaders. It was only natural, then, that support for ecumenism should decline among those persons most threatened by church union. True ecumenical believers, however, have been willing to push on, in spite of threats to their livelihood.

The cutback in church programs during the 1960s closed some theological schools and caused mergers of others, and encouraged cooperative support for social-action programs and missions. Within the last decade it has become fairly common for Roman Catholic priests to study in Protestant theological schools and Protestants, in Roman Catholic schools. Indeed, some Roman Catholic schools are merging facilities with Protestant schools in expression of an inherent unity in Christian institutions.

Modern media, particulaly television, promote an intimacy of feeling and understanding, if not agreement, among persons widely separated in geography, nationality, and ecumenical persuasion. National and international travel, made possible in the jet age, promote widespread interaction and observation between differing peoples and institutions. And so, while there continues to be some resistance to organic union by denominational servants, ecumenicity of mind has not been and cannot be restrained in an increasingly aware and sophisticated laity. Probably the vast majority of modern people—even those who belong to religious groups—do not believe strongly in religious denominations anymore. This seems to be the case even when family tradition has been strongly associated with a given religious group for generations. The modern man may have grown up in a Baptist family; attended a Presbyterian Sunday school; joined a Disciples senior high fellowship; dated an Episcopalian and a Quaker; run around with a member of the Assembly of God, a Christian Scientist, and a Pentecostal; and married an Eastern Orthodox. He may play golf with a Roman Catholic; have Jewish neighbors; and his children attend the nearest church, which may happen to be Lutheran. His story is duplicated in a slightly different version by both his brothers and his sisters. He might express it this way.

> I no longer believe in the superiority of my religious group over any other. I am aware that all groups have their contributions to make and that all have their unique blindnesses. I honor my religion, and I believe it is right for me, but I can honor the validity of many other groups as well, and I believe in working together in every way possible.[7]

Organic union of churches may proceed slowly, haltingly, and even slip backward occasionally, but the ecumenical spirit brought about by interaction of lay and clerical Christian men and women, the vicarious interaction through media, and the indwelling single Spirit of God have brought about a genuine unity of understanding that, given time, will sweep away ecclesiastical structures that forbid unity of action. Increasingly, those denominational institutions that justify their very existence on the basis of minor differences from other churches will be subsumed by the unifying Holy Spirit. As Christians of different denominational camps undertake common tasks in the community, their theological disputes, often unheard and meaningless to laymen, will wane. Denominational labels will continue for a time—perhaps forever—but Christians increasingly will think of the Christian church as a single entity. We will think not of the Lutheran Church, or of the Catholic Church, or of the Assemblies of God, but of Christians in St. Louis or Boston or Louisville, or of Christians in metropolitan areas.

As thoughtful Christians examine the multiplicity of church buildings, with the attendant staggering economic, spiritual, and aesthetic costs, they will find ways for common use of a single building by several congregations. Christians who more and more find themselves one in the Spirit, touched directly or indirectly by the new Pentecostal spirit, will find ways of living, working, sharing, and praising together. It is a rare opportunity for the ministry to recognize what has happened and what will happen in expression of inherent Christian unity. It is not likely that we ever will be fully together theologically, but the day of sectarian denominationalism was buried in the media avalanche and the neo-Pentecostal renewal of the 1960s and 1970s. A ministry thinking otherwise must sooner or later discover that it is ice-skating on an unfrozen lake.

THE CHURCH—1929–1980

In October 1929, the stock market crash initiatied the Great Depression that lasted throughout the 1930s. The economic depression was associated with religious depression, as churches suffered along with the rest of the nation. Memberships dropped, budgets were slashed, benevolent and missionary enterprises were stranded, and professional church workers discharged as churches and chapels closed for lack of money. Newer and smaller religious groups, particularly Pentecostals, however, prospered, feeding upon the economically depressed classes who either had no church home or were unable to economically sustain membership in a regular church. They, too, however, needed a ministry. Before mainline churches could recover from the depression or the newer churches could assimilate their gains, the United States entered World War II. Churches of most denominations turned their energies to the war effort, and other programs were "put on hold."

A great majority of the young men of the nation, along with not a few young women, entered the armed forces, had overseas service in both Christian and non-Christian lands, and returned home with vastly broadened views. Many other Americans entered defense industries to do their part in the war effort. A veritable cultural revolution resulted when the GIs and defense industry citizens sought to return to business as usual after the war.

The United States emerged from World War II not only victorious, but with such a sense of invincibility that the afterglow lasted until the American troops bogged down in the rice paddies of

Vietnam. The Eisenhower years were quiet, prosperous, stable times. The Korean War was over, and Joseph McCarthy had not succeeded in destroying the nation. The economy was prosperous. The GIs were home, married, having children, and looking for moral and spiritual guidance for their families. They filled the churches, and the 1950s and early 1960s were a time of unprecedented congregational growth and participation.

Protestant church membership peaked in the late 1950s and then leveled off. Catholic membership growth continued until the mid-1960s. In 1958, approximately 49 percent of the population of the United States reported attending church during the average week: Catholics reported 74 percent; Protestants, 44 percent. Church incomes rose and growing suburbs gave rise to new church development.

But since the mid-1960s, participation, if not membership, in churches has taken a sharp downturn. This does not mean, however, that membership declined proportionately with participation. Mainline Protestant denominations did show an unprecedented decline in membership. Catholicism did not lose as many members, but regular church attendance dropped to 56 percent by 1975. Average Protestant attendance declined, settling at 37 percent in the mid-1970s. New church development slowed to almost nothing. On the other hand, several conservative denominations continued to grow at significant rates, including a 14 percent increase for Southern Baptists and 31 percent for the Assemblies of God, in the decade between 1965 and 1975.[8]

This then is the pattern of church development between 1950 and 1980; during those years several issues surfaced that called for the attention of our preachers. We turn now to a consideration of those matters.

THE MATURATION OF THE BLACK CHURCH

The growth of the black church in the period following the Civil War came at a time when the United States was unable or unwilling to implement the newly enacted thirteenth, fourteenth, and fifteenth amendments, which provided full citizenship for blacks. There was a steady rise in the size and strength of black churches, as they provided not only spiritual succor but opportunities for self-expression and places of leadership in the only institution totally controlled by blacks. The church was the most powerful social and political institution for blacks, and this continues to be true even today—much of the leadership of the total black community still comes from the church.

Until well into the twentieth century many black pastors preached an otherworldly kingdom of God—a kingdom literally out of this world and having little or nothing to do with the social and economic conditions here. This hope-of-glory-to-come religion appealed to black people, who were barely surviving the oppressive conditions under which they lived. Churches became places of celebration—celebration of escape from dehumanizing and depersonalizing direct and institutional racism. Following the "Jesus glory road" led to escape from this vale of tears to the redeemed life, where there would be no more sorrow and where there would be pearly gates, streets of gold, and long white robes.

In such a climate, Booker T. Washington (1856–1915) emerged as the primary national black spokesman. He advocated an accommodation to segregation strategy. W.E.B. DuBois (1868–1963), a Harvard doctoral graduate, led a revolt against the Booker philosophy and in 1907, aided in the founding of the Niagara Movement, which swiftly gained support and developed into the National Association for the Advancement of Colored People (NAACP) in 1909. The rise of an organized black protest movement became feasible only with the growth of black populations in the great industrial centers of the North—Chicago, Detroit, New York, Boston. Thousands of people had moved to those areas from farms, villages, and towns of the South in the first years of the twentieth century, and they took their churches with them, meeting in stores and other rented buildings of the cities. From this modest beginning, very gradual but definite strides toward fuller black citizenship were made over the next four decades, through court battles, executive orders, marches, urban riots, and a strengthening prophetic voice from the black pulpit.

From its earliest days the black church, which was overwhelmingly Protestant—usually Baptist or Methodist—helped its members adjust to the economic realities of being black in a white man's world, by the formation of cooperatives for housing, insurance, job referral, and an assortment of farming and industrial enterprises on a small scale. In their churches blacks found expression, release, hope, and an odds-on chance for a place of leadership. Especially in the freer churches it was not uncommon for a congregation to have three or four major choirs, a male usher board, a female usher board, and up to a half dozen ministers of various levels of authority in the pulpit. This provided many opportunities for places of leadership.

The black minister has been and still is a supremely authoritative figure, both in the church and in the community. He is looked to for advice on medicine, politics, taxation, and family life, as well as theology. Indeed, the imposing image of the black preacher lures a significant number of young blacks to take a serious look at the opportunity for leadership through the ministerial office.

The embryonic black revolution was aided by the growth of the NAACP and the limited success of specific protest movements such as Marcus Garvey's Universal Negro Improvement Association, popularly known as the "Back to Africa" movement, which was active from about 1916 to 1923. Black awareness, evoked by Garvey, helped promote a sense of dignity in the black church, and it began to be more concerned about the here and now. Black churches have become socially concerned, in part because black citizens have become people of social concern, and black ministers, in many cases, have had to run to keep up with their people.

The late Martin Luther King, Jr. well represents the emerging prophetic voice of the twentieth-century black pulpit. He was at his best in challenging the white community: "We shall match your capacity to inflict suffering by our capacity to endure suffering. We shall meet your physical force by soul force. Do with us what you will, we shall continue to love you."[9] King, of course, spoke from a black pulpit, where prophetic preaching understandably received a warm response. He found, however, many ways to challenge the white community directly, especially through media coverage of his protests and through his writing.

By 1965, King was generally recognized as the conscience of America, and he gave heart to thousands of other black preachers seeking to follow his very courageous example. It is noteworthy that the black pulpit, in contrast to the white pulpit, is in a relatively advantageous position from which to present a prophetic message. It generally does not have a vested interest at stake when it cries out against police brutality, preferential treatment against minorities in employment, exploitative absentee landlords, and the like. The elders, deacons, and stewards who are the ecclesiastical bosses in black churches usually do not manage corporations, banks, or industries. On the other hand, middle- and upper-class white churches are likely to be controlled by a board of directors that tends to mute the prophetic voice of the church.

The gentle but potent force of direct militant nonviolence hardened with the shooting of James Meredith as he walked from Memphis to Jackson, Mississippi, in June, 1965. "Black power" became the slogan of the Negro revolution. Following this new spirit, forty black churchmen met in Bethel African Methodist Episcopal Church in Harlem in July 1966, admitting that "too often the Negro church has steered its members away from the reign of God in *this world* to a distorted and complacent view of *an other worldly* conception of God's power."[10] For them it was imperative that the black churches discontinue their basic accommodation of white supremacy.

Martin Luther King, Jr.'s theology of reconciliation lost influence as Negro theologians became black theologians and took up the banner of black power. Albert B. Cleage, Jr. and James H. Cone became major spokesmen for a new theology of black liberation. The basic issue is black freedom: Any doctrine that makes for black freedom is the gospel of Jesus Christ; if a doctrine is against or indifferent to black power, then it is the work of the Antichrist.[11] Major J. Jones and J. Deotis Roberts developed a theology of hope, a competing black theology that also addressed black awareness, liberation, and self-affirmation. Jones and Roberts stress the central Christian theme of reconciliation and suggest black responsibility for teaching the larger Christian community some basic lessons in living the Christian life of love for all humankind. They represent a blend of the militant theology of liberation and King's radical militant nonviolent theology and method of reconciliation.

Meanwhile, the oppressed and distressed inner-city blacks continued to respond heartily to the otherworldly attractions of sects and cults, which generally failed to address either racism or liberation. Father Divine, Daddy Grace, the Reverend Ike, Marcus Garvey, and others, all have presented movements offering hope of escape from the ghetto jungles of our cities.

Generally, black churches in America have a continuing record of strong emphasis on preaching that is faithful to the basic doctrines of the Christian faith, including the kerygma. They are now also in a generally concerted prophetic voice, but unfortunately, their messages usually do not reach the people who are in a position to correct the ills of their concern. The black ministry must find channels of communication to those seats of institutional power and wealth that have the ability to help.

For a final word on the black church, let it be noted that one is now more likely to find aggressive, interesting, compelling, biblical preaching in the black church than in any other segment of Christendom in America. It would be most enlightening and inspirational for the typical white minister to take a few Sundays out of his own pulpit and sit under the preaching of the average Protestant black minister.

THE ACCEPTANCE OF CATHOLICS

The Roman Catholic Church in the United States has been both blessed and hobbled by massive immigrations that brought growth to the church, but language, liturgical, and cultural problems to the priesthood. As the church sought to adapt to the American culture, it raised the ire of the papacy by adopting non-European patterns of behavior and thought. In 1898 the "heresy" of Americanism was officially condemned. Oddly enough, while Rome viewed the church in the United States as too American, non-Catholic Americans viewed American Catholics as too Roman—not sufficiently American. The Catholic membership had grown quite rapidly until about 1925 but then, like most churches, its growth rate slowed during the depression. Between 1926 and 1936 it grew only 7 percent, as compared to 18.3 percent in the previous ten years.[12] But the revival of interest in religion following World War II spurred new growth, and Catholics numbered 32 million in the early 1950s, with over 116,000 converts to the faith in 1953.

The formal opening of the North American College within Vatican City in 1953 spoke well for Catholicism in the United States. The towering walls, spacious corridors, and comfortable rooms clearly indicated great American Catholic wealth and power. Roman Catholic clergy in America had come into their own.[13] It had been but forty-five years since the day in 1908 when Pope Pius X brought an end to the missionary status of the Roman Catholic Church in the United States. Before that time, the European-head-quartered Society for the Propagation of the Faith had long supported the American Catholic Church as a mission of Rome. By 1957 the mass immigration had come to an end and the flow of money was reversed, with 65 percent of the total budget of the society coming from the United States. Also, by 1960, Americans composed one-ninth of the total Roman Catholic foreign missionary force.[14] Catholics developed the largest private parochial system in the world, and in 1964 there were more than 6 million students in American Catholic schools. Approximately 50,000 students preparing for the priesthood were enrolled in 596 seminaries.

The Catholic hierarchy took a firm hand in the area of racial justice by the 1950s. Work before that time had generally followed a segregated pattern throughout the United States, but in 1947 the Catholic schools of St. Louis ended segregation, as did those in Washington, D.C. and Raleigh, North Carolina, in 1953. Churches and hospitals in those dioceses were also integrated.

After World War II Catholics strengthened their intellectual interests and their scholarship contributions increased. Up until that time American Catholics had been considerably occupied by continuing immigrant assimilation and the attendant problem of being viewed as a foreign church by the established white Anglo-Saxon Protestant mentality.

The general revival of religion in the 1950s in America was marked by the dynamic spirited preaching of Roman Catholic Fulton J. Sheen (1895–1979) and the writings of Trappist mystic Thomas Merton (1915–1968). Bishop Sheen ranked with Billy Graham and Norman Vincent Peale in his ability to popularize his particular brand of religion.

The growing maturity of American Roman Catholics reflected a greater emphasis on intellectual pursuits, a stronger role of the laity in the church, and an increased sense of responsibility to society in general. These concerns were reinforced by "caretaker" Pontiff John XXIII and the Second Vatican Council. Pope John's openness to the world rubbed off on the American Catholic Church, permitting them to shed most of their immigrant image and to begin to live and work with Americans of other faiths—even those of considerable dissimilarity.[15]

A revival of interest in the improvement of Catholic preaching began with the 1936 publication of Father Joseph Jungmann's *The Good News and the Proclamation of the Faith*. Immediately following World War II a number of order and diocesan priests pursued advanced studies in rhetoric at Northwestern, Ohio State, Wisconsin, and other schools. Like the Church Fathers before them, they were going back to the fountain of secular rhetoric to learn the basics of communication for application in proclamation of the Word. In 1958, in order to improve the preaching apostolate, the Catholic Homiletic Society was founded by Father Joseph M. Connors, a Divine Word priest. The establishment of the Word of God Institute in Washington, D.C., which publishes preaching aids and holds conferences on preaching; the widespread use of experienced Protestant homileticians to teach in major Catholic seminaries; and a lively business in several varieties of homily services—all give evidence of growing concern for effective communication of the Word from Catholic pulpits. This renewal received encouragement when Vatican Council II underscored anew the obligatory place of the homily in the regular liturgy of the church. To aid in this thrust, the *Decree of Ministry and Life of Priests* mandates that a series of courses in homiletics be included in the seminary curriculum so that priests, upon finishing professional training, will be better prepared to preach.[16]

Weekly attendance at mass has currently dropped to some 50 percent of the Catholic population, but that is still a staggering number of people seeking priestly services of Word and Sacrament. There are now some one thousand fewer priests in the United States than there were ten years ago, however, and no remedy for this situation is readily apparent, since Catholic seminary enrollment is less than a third of its size ten years ago. The shortage of priests will apparently get worse before it gets better.

The current women's movement seeks to open the full ministry of Word and Sacrament in Catholicism to women, and successful efforts in this regard could, of course, relieve the shortage of priests. That option, however, does not have much chance of success in the immediate future.

In summary, the Roman Catholic Church is now broadly accepted as a genuine part of the American scene, but its effectiveness at present is hampered by organizational and disciplinary disarray, and these difficulties are compounded by a growing shortage of priests.

THE TURBULENT 1960s

The easy, complacent Eisenhower years, marked by religiosity and burgeoning churches, faded quickly into the turbulent 60s. Then, even with vast natural resources, marvelous technological advances, expansive ideals, opportunities for college education for essentially all ambitious youth, and well-populated churches, society seemed to come apart at the seams.

Perennially optimistic, America began to sense that everything was not OK in its world, especially in its own backyard. Everything went wrong—the Bay of Pigs fiasco, the Vietnam police action, the assassinations of the Kennedys and Martin Luther King, Jr., mounting unrest, discontent, and burnings and bombings in the cities. And while the civil rights movement won some early gains, the racial crises in the cities did not stop. Black power took over leadership of the black revolution, ejecting whites, and some long, hot summers followed. The Supreme Court ruling on one-man-one-vote cut into the political power of the Protestant establishment. Another ruling made compulsory prayer and Bible reading in public school unconstitutional, much to the distress of a majority of Americans.

In 1960, Catholic John Kennedy had broken the Protestant monopoly on the presidency, only to be assassinated in 1963. The nation and the world joined in the media-orchestrated concert of grief. Aged Pope John XXIII called Vatican Council II in 1963, ending the four-hundred-year-old Counter-Reformation and setting other sweeping reforms in motion in the Christian world.

Following the counsel of his military advisers, President Lyndon

Johnson ordered the bombing of North Vietnam in February 1965, and in that year our troop level there was raised to 200,000. By 1969, more than 500,000 of our youth were in Vietnam and chronic divisiveness in America was becoming critical—even grave. Old bases of authority—the government, the home, the school, and even the church—were widely questioned, as clear gaps between ideals and performance were evident. The media, especially television, were making an unprecented impact on social consciousness and greatly speeded up the impact of events on the public mind. Those years were also a time in which a college education was increasingly normative for ambitious American young people, and this made traditional religious values subject to a more careful analysis before acceptance.

It was a time of philosophical insurrection in America; it was a time when, occasioned by the Vietnam war, at least some Americans began to see our country as others in the world had seen it for some time. An idealistic syndrome of sensitivity to human ills and an effort to minimize restraint on complete personal freedom appeared to be at the core of a number of violently controverted issues. Combined, these issues were all quite related and formed a cohesive and coherent whole. They centered around the black revolution, the youth rebellion, the growing demand for equality, the general rejection of an authoritarian culture, the opposition to the spread of additional power abroad, a favoring of the natural environment over commercial profit (ecology), a radical new approach to moral values, and the feminist attack on masculine domination.[17] These extreme humanistic issues had been in the making for years—some of them for generations. Now they were coming to a common time of focus. No longer would we pursue a naïve creed that all things are resolvable if only one works hard and knows the right people. Gone were the days of the simplistic optimism that our country's material future would inevitably continue to grow bigger and better. This was a vital and dramatic break in the long line of assured self-perception that the United States had held, essentially from its inception. Our nation suffered a profound psychic and philosophical shock when all these events and issues converged in the decade of the 1960s. A widespread sense of national failure in relation to humane issues resulted, in spite of almost unlimited production and personal wealth.

Now, what does this have to do with preaching? The churches were made up of people—citizens of the American society—who perhaps for the first time saw themselves as something less than generous and genteel philanthropists, seeking to share their largess with unfortunate fellow human beings at home and abroad. Many began to see some of the basic inconsistencies and hypocrisies of American society, and they realized that, in the main, the church—Catholic, Protestant, and Eastern Orthodox—supported the status quo that bound so many in chains of poverty, ignorance, prejudice, chauvinism, and gerrymandering. The church had baptized this country and had set it in one of the finest seats in the temple.

It was then that church people, lay and professional, Protestant and Catholic—began to realize the terrible impotence of the American church in its prophetic ministry. The church simply was not dealing with the "now" world. It had divided the kingdom and had limited God's redemptive forces to purely personal and otherworldly spheres. This realization of the church's isolation from prophetic issues drove disillusioned members from her ranks. Other church people of the conservative position were encouraged that the church was not involved with secular matters and found even more time and money to support her. Mainline denominations declined in membership, but dating from the mid-1960s, neoevangelical and fundamentalist groups achieved a new strength and growth.

Out of this crisis of spirit, many Americans developd a new attitude for dealing with other people. This attitude was a realistic, healthy, but touchy skepticism about what to expect from persons and institutions, sacred and secular. Sydney Ahlstrom delineates three categories of attitudes that emerged at varying intensities from this crisis. They were (1) acceptance of naturalism or secularism as a way of interpreting life; (2) awareness of the wide gap between the ideals and the performance of political, social, educational, and ecclesiastical institutions; and (3) doubt as to the ability of our institutions to correct the profound ills of society.[18] These ideas were basic, unstructured, even subliminal premises, on which a great number of thoughtful persons operated. These premises began to guide church people and non-church people alike, often producing a sober, pessimistic skepticism toward the ideals and teachings of the church. Development of such attitudes portended rough days ahead for the preacher, for such ideas seem antithetical to the essential nature and gospel of the church.

WOMEN AND THE CHURCH

With the women's liberation movement pressing to remove all hindrance to full female participation in personhood, it is only natural that women should seek full acceptance into the full Christian ministry. The American church has an extremely spotty record on the issue of ordination of women. Before the rise of the Holiness and Pentecostal groups, primarily in this century, women preachers were quite rare, except in the freer churches such as the Quakers and the semiecclesiatical organizations such as the Salvation Army. Rebecca Collins spoke at Quaker meetings as early as 1696, and since that time the Society of Friends has often been ministered to by women. Evangeline Booth, wife of the founder of the Salvation Army, strongly influenced that organization through her pulpit eloquence. Her record shows her to be one of the strongest women preachers in modern church history. Presbyterians now readily accept women for ordination, but their record over the years is representative of the negative attitude of mainline Protestants. The Newark Presbytery, in 1876, convicted Elijah R. Craven, pastor of Third Presbyterian Church in Newark, New Jersey, for permitting women to preach and teach from the pulpit. The Synod of New Jersey and the General Assembly sustained his conviction on the basis that the Scriptures forbade women to speak in church.[19]

An effort to allow Episcopal women priests, pushed for several years in bitterness and controversy, culminated in the ordination of women to the full priesthood in January, 1977. The Lambeth Conference of the Anglican Church in Canterbury, England, in 1978, sustained the ordination of women and thus jeopardized the ongoing ecumenical dialogue with Roman Catholic and Eastern Orthodox churches.

When the free churches began to ordain women in the nineteenth century, it went almost unnoticed by the Roman and Orthodox Christians, for at that time there was no hint of church union or cooperation in ministry. Now, with ecumenical dialogue, it is a matter of quite urgent concern. Approximately two-thirds of the women clergy of the United States are in Pentecostal churches or organizations such as the Salvation Army; only 17 percent are found in major Protestant denominations. Only three of the ten major denominations that now ordain women, did so prior to 1956—American Baptist, Christian, and the United Church of Christ.[20]

In the Roman Catholic and Eastern Orthodox churches, women foresee no quick success in their quest for full priesthood. Pope John Paul II, in his 1979 visit to the United States, spoke strongly on the conservative side of issues that divide the American Catholic Church—birth control, married priests, women priests, divorce, homosexuality, and abortion. Liberals had not expected him to endorse women priests, but had hoped that he at least would refrain from stirring up the issue during his visit.[21] But Elizabeth Achtemeier, visiting professor of homiletics and hermeneutics at Union Theological Seminary in Richmond, Virginia, a Presbyterian institution, predicts that, barring any large-scale distortion of their ministries, women eventually will be given full acceptance in all branches of the Christian church. She believes that the church will find it increasingly difficult to resist the Spirit, if women keep their own motives clear.[22]

All of this is to say that more and more women are responding to their perception of God's call into the ministry. Perhaps they have been hearing that call for a long time, but barriers have discouraged them from following it. Women are graduating from colleges with high honors, outshining their male counterparts in language studies, biblical studies, and theological and philosophical studies, and are seeking every opportunity for professional church vocations, ordination, and full ministry. While they do not have a long tradition of pulpit eloquence, their talent, persistence, and motivation, as demonstrated by their excellent seminary records, will thrust large numbers of highly qualified women into the preaching market. A little competition between the sexes can only help improve the quality of preaching.

THE ELECTRIC CHURCH

At this time, the "electric church" broadcasts an amazing number of radio and television programs. The sermon format is usually bypassed for talk-show type interviews, and entertainment in a religious frame of language and thought. Occasionally a program may take the form of an analysis of selected current topics, using a vocabulary of appropriate religious terms.

Now some 1,100 radio stations and 25 television stations broadcast religious messages almost exclusively. In 1979, religious radio stations opened at the rate of about one a week, and religious TV stations, about one a month.[23] Heavy capital investment is required to build broadcast facilities: Construction alone costs a minimum of $200,000 for a radio station and $2 million for a television station. This does not include licensing, staffing, and operational costs. However, the *Wall Street Journal* has estimated that religious broadcasting generates a cash flow of some $.5 billion a year.[24]

The National Religious Broadcasters, headed by Ben Armstrong, claim that they reach a regular audience of 114 million radio listeners and 15 million TV viewers. The Christian Broadcasting Network currently feeds 130 commerical and 4,000 cable stations in North America, while Oral Roberts' broadcasts are watched by as many as 62 million people worldwide. Religious broadcasting, then, is a very big operation. Apparently, however, while some denominations and church councils sponsor such broadcasting, a very large part of the most visible aspects are ventures of individuals, private nonprofit corporations, or single congregations. In an average week 47 percent of the American population switches on radio or television for at least one religious program, while only 42 percent attend a church service. It would be interesting to know how many of those who tune in religious broadcasting also attend church.

The overwhelming majority of the religious radio and TV stations are owned by evangelical Protestants; thus most of the programs are Protestant and evangelical. Costs are often prohibitive, especially in television, and mainline denominations generally have invested little in television programming. Consequently, their telecasts most often are free public service programs on local stations or rare, network-financed programs in the Sunday morning "ghetto."

Thus far, the electric church, as a nondenominational activity, has not sought to build itself into a definitive church. On the other hand, it does have something of an invisible structure and routine. Its adherents do not know one another or share in fellowship, except as a few might get together to watch a particular evangelist/enter-tainer/showman. People belong to the electric church by turning to the right place on the dial and mailing in their contributions; quite often they begin to use some of the jargon of their favorite religious broadcaster.

Pat Robertson's "700 Club" of the Christian Broadcasting Network (CBN) of Virginia Beach is one of the continuing popular successes of the electric church. One of its early innovations was counseling. This gives viewers an opportunity to talk by telephone with a "700 Club" counselor in one of the seventy-five local centers across the nation, all operating around the clock. Typical is the Spiritual Life Center in the Dallas-Fort Worth metroplex, which uses a team of eight to twelve counselors, from a pool of approximately two hundred active volunteers. These volunteers work while the "700 Club" is on the air, and a skeleton crew staffs the phones during the rest of the day. During an average ninety-minute show, a counselor handles five to ten calls—listening, advising, and praying. [25] Currently the "700 Club" is aired in all 50 states and in 22 foreign countries, over some 200 TV stations and 150 radio outlets; 4,000 communities receive it by cable TV. Pat Robertson, the moving force behind CBN, has parlayed the operation into the largest syndicate of satellite-transmitted programs in the United States. He plans a competitive fourth television network, through which affiliates will receive forty hours of programming a week. The religious programs produced by CBN will be the core of offerings, but wholesome family news, sports, information, comedy and variety shows, and probably even a Christian soap opera, will be included.

Something of a pattern for CBN affiliates has been established by KXTX in Dallas, a UHF television station. It, incidentally, is owned by CBN and can be used to test acceptance of new programs or formats. General manager Robert Baerwolf reports that KXTX's format contains much more than the "700 Club" and other Christian programs. It telecasts "Father Knows Best," "The Brady Bunch," "The Partridge Family," and the like. These shows build audiences and keep the independent station alive financially. They serve as bait to attract viewers into the electric church. "When we ran only Christian shows," says Baerwolf, "we were doing a pretty good job of edifying the church, but we were not reaching unsaved people." Prior to diversifying the programming, some 30,000 households tuned in to KXTX each week. Now that the programming is family-oriented, some 600,000 households listen each week. [26]

Traditional ecclesiastics express concern that the electric church is pulling people away from congregational participation and substituting an anonymous commitment to a radio or television program. Researchers have discovered difficulty in channeling media- and mass-evangelism converts into church membership. Studies of the Institute for American Church Government, released in January 1978, suggest that mass evangelism is simply not now an effective method of increasing church membership. Of thousands of decisions registered by the Campus Crusade in the "I found it" campaign, only 3 percent of the "converts" were ever incorpoated into a local church. Who knows how many people are growing increasingly satisfied to remain outside the church and receive their religion exclusively through an electronic box? [27]

Some elements of the electric church have clear but unusual nonecclesiastical goals—goals that are certainly within reasonable, if not traditional, bounds of the kingdom of God. Doubtless some celebrities of the electric church are building fame, power, and on occasion, wealth for themselves. To some degree they are substituting a phantom, invisible, nonpeopled relationship to a television image for the church of real people, with real needs, who share together in a redemptive face-to-face fellowship. The church as a community of believers has always been a central part of the Christian faith and life. It is where sins are confessed and forgiveness, regeneration, and spiritual sustenance are found in a continuing, helping fellowship. Television, especially, is allowing talented, attractive preachers/talkers to establish a compelling, personal, one-on-one relationship with millions of viewers. Successful programmers in the electric church have studied and adopted techniques of commercial television. They must be given credit for adapting this most powerful of all media to the use of the gospel. As we have said, the problem arises, however, when the individual viewer permits the electric church to substitute for the fellowship of his own church. The local church—the community of believers—is an essential part of Christian faith and life. The electric church can never substitute, nor does it seem to try to substitute, for the personal, redemptive encounter in the live fellowship of the faithful, with its resulting impact in the community.

The quality of communication in the services of the Christian church has long suffered from painful comparison with the broadcast media. Until ministers/priests improve their communicative ability; until church music and church architecture are transformed; until the services impart the interesting and stimulating experiences necessary for a media-oriented society, the church will continue to fare poorly in its communication responsibility.

Mainline churches have mounted halfhearted efforts in both radio and television to compete with the programming of the "big three" networks. The church programming that has adopted the professional standards of the broadcasting industry has fared well, but most has not, and is exciting only to a favored few in the inner circle of the sponsoring denominations. At least the leaders of the electric church have wrestled with the challenge of media, particularly television, and are increasingly successful in reaching millions well beyond their own denominations. These efforts cost money, and each of the religious broadcasters, whether it be Jerry Falwell, Robert Schuler, Oral Roberts, Pat Robertson, Billy Graham, Rex Humbard, Jim Bakker, or some other, has his own particular project, over and above program expenses, for which he seeks support. With Pat Robertson, for example, it is CBN University with graduate programs in communication and law, and a competitive fourth television network. Unquestionably, if CBN, through shrewd business management, can develop a competitive network, it could have a radical impact for good on American society. Up to this point, no mainline denomination seems to have made any successful effort at establishing a wholesome family-oriented network of television programming.

Most of the programming of the electric church, and probably the most successful in numbers of listeners, is not formal preaching, but talk, entertainment, and testimony. A few liturgical services, offering breezy sermonettes by commandingly attractive, camera-wise, master-of-ceremony type preachers also compete well for listeners. Whether these are lasting new ways of communicating the

Word is not entirely clear, but millions of people do listen to religious messages over radio and television. The lesson of the electric church is that the church—a church willing to present a gospel with a cross, for the Christian as well as for the Christ—can use radio and television to aid in its communication of the Word. The gospel can be packaged in a style and form to meet the broadcasting standards of listener and viewer. Any effort following less than professional models of production is almost certain to bring failure to the program, and criticism of the gospel.

THE PENTECOSTALS

Pentecostals as a separate religious body appeared early in this century and for some three generations stood separate and apart from the rest of the Christian church structure. Now in the United States there are more than 6 million people in Pentecostal denominations, not counting those who are widely dispersed in the non-Pentecostal denominations. There are some 30 million Pentecostals worldwide, most of them in third-world countries. Modern Pentecostals, both black and white, trace their beginnings to a small black church on Azusa Street in Los Angeles, under the leadership of a black American preacher, William J. Seymour.[28]

The terms Pentecostal and charismatic are often used interchangeably, but old-timers seem to prefer the term *Pentecostal* while newcomers lean toward *charismatic*. A slight difference sometimes is implied in the use of the term Pentecostal, in the sense that it indicates a lower status, rougher-cut, Protestant charismatic. A distinction is sometimes made between "hard" and "soft" charismatics; the hard variety views non-Pentecostal Christians as less-than-first-class people, who are not fully saved. The soft charismatics follow the guidelines of the general Pentecostal movement, but are more open in accepting non-Pentecostal Christians as full brothers and sisters in the Lord.[29]

Pentecostalism, contained for three generations in its own denominations, spilled over ecclesiastical lines during the 1950s and gifts of the Spirit, often including "speaking in tongues," began to show up in mainline denominations. This movement, now known as neo-Pentecostalism, or the charismatic movement, is based on the commonality of baptism in the Holy Spirit. The events at St. Mark's Episcopal Church in Van Nuys, California, in 1960 were especially notable in the spread of Pentecostalism. The rector, Dennis Bennett, experienced what he reported to be a baptism of the Holy Spirit and the gift of tongues, and he made general testimony of this occurrence to his congregation. After that the walls came tumbling down, and the charismatic movement spread more widely into mainline denominations—Episcopal, Methodist, Presbyterian, Baptist, and Lutheran—and into Roman Catholicism, particularly after 1966.[30] The story of the happening in Van Nuys received national press coverage in both *Time* and *Newsweek* and helped to give some cohesion to other events that had been taking place in isolated, usually unreported, incidents. Bennett gained some national status and became an important factor in the growth and spread of the charismatic renewal in America.

During the 1950s the Full Gospel Businessmen's Fellowship International (FGBMFI) was established by Demos Shakarian as a nondenominational Pentecostal prayer breakfast-luncheon fellowship. It has served as a cohesive force in Pentecostalism, drawing together, from both Pentecostal and non-Pentecostal churches, men, and occasionally women, who are seeking to share their blessings in the Spirit with one another and with the "unbaptized." The FGBMFI added a strong ecumenical emphasis, some respectablity, and some financial strength to Pentecostalism. All this helped to shape the charismatic movement into an entity more palatable to the non-Pentecostal world.

For the first half of the twentieth century Pentecostalism had been a sanctuary for the down-and-out and the disinherited, and had generated numbers of independent denominations. Then it began to penetrate older Protestant churches, but without causing the converts to defect from those churches. After about 1960, the new baptisms in the Spirit began to appear in elite congregations, and while they regularly met opposition, they did not generally produce schisms or new churches. And as those new in the Spirit found joy and a personal relationship with God, as contrasted with the spiritual apathy they had previously known, churches softened and on occasion were tolerant and even accepting toward the "baptism."

The growth of Pentecostalism in traditional churches is illustrated by the Presbyterian Charismatic Communion (PCC), which, in early 1980, has active support from 900 ministers and 5,000 laity. Over the years since 1966, when PCC was founded, some 3,000 Presbyterian ministers have actively subscribed their support. Brick Bradford, general secretary of the organization, after widespread travel and observation, suggests that there are 100,000 to 120,000 "baptized in the Holy Spirit" Presbyterians in the United States.

After 1966, Pentecostalism showed up more frequently in Catholicism. Several explanations have been offered as to why this occurred, but whatever the reason, it found an even more ready response there than among Protestants. Perhaps one explanation is that, unlike many Protestant churches, Roman Catholic authorities, who function in a strong ecclesiastical structure, were less threatened by charismatics and thus less uncompromising in opposition.

Baptism in the Spirit, then, has moved uptown. It is now neo-Pentecostal or charismatic. Its followers generally no longer come from conditions of sociocultural disruption or low status, or because of dissatisfaction. The neo-Pentecostals, whether Protestant or Catholic, now tend not to be divisive. Their meetings are much more orderly than those of the old-time Pentecostals, with less emotion displayed in receiving the gifts of the Spirit. The private experience of the Spirit is regarded as equally as valid as the public display of its manifestations.[31]

So what does all this mean for the preacher? Certainly it should be comforting for those in the ministry who have long given lip service to partnership with the Spirit in preaching, to see evidence that the Holy Spirit is indeed a living presence and partner in the communicaton of the Word. Plainly, the Spirit underwrites a genuine joy in the Lord, as Christians express their faith unreservedly in public and private worship. Unfortunately, some charismatic ministers have so given over the service, including the sermon, to the control of the Spirit that they have abandoned their own responsibility for preaching preparation and exercise of their own God-given gifts. The work of preaching is a collaboration with the Holy Spirit, but collaboration is working together, or co-laboring, and thus means the exercise of the full being and effort of the preacher. On the other hand, preachers often profess dependence upon the Holy Spirit, but they show reluctance to use

God's anointing power to enable them to speak. It is the power of the Holy Spirit that frees and fires the preacher for proclaiming the Word. The truly anointed-of-God preacher can sense when that freedom and fire is present and when it is absent, and so can a congregation of believers. Simulation indicates artificiality, and the people of the congregation know when that certain something is missing. It is the Holy Spirit who brings illumination and transformation and makes the Word of God come alive as the gospel is being proclaimed. As this Word comes alive in the listening and "faithing" congregation, gifts of the Holy Spirit will be manifest decently and in order, as God directs. The unobtrusive minister will not be found seeking to confine, or to direct how, when, or where the Holy Spirit will work.

The preaching ministry is a vocation of cooperation with God through the Holy Spirit. Indeed, the primary element in preaching is that which is behind, in, and beside the preacher—the reality of a God who speaks in and through the preacher. Those uncomfortable with this arrangement, or hesitant to draw upon the resources of the Spirit, will suffer in their preaching ministry. Preaching cannot rely on human strength alone, for the purposes of preaching cannot be accomplished solely through even the best human rhetoric. Conversely, God is not likely to infuse the preaching of one who fails to put forth his or her own best effort.

CULTS AND THE CHURCH

Following the breakdown of customary social structures during the 1960s, amidst civil rights disturbances, protests against the war, and a general lack of confidence in our basic institutions, young people looked to nontraditional means for salvation. Pseudogods, long since exorcised by orthodox Christianity, were born anew, and many students, proud of their rational approach to life in other ways, became fascinated by incantations, incense, rituals, drugs, and even the irrational. In cultic expression, this fascination went far into astrology, Satan worship, witchcraft (black and white), or into a spin-off of more traditional religion, such as the Jesus movement, the Children of God, or the Unification Church. The Maharishi of the Spiritual Regeneration Movement, Swami Yoganda of the Self-realization Fellowship, and other pundits from the East found fertile soil for their gospel of inner peace, cosmic consciousness, and self-fulfillment.

Many young people felt cut adrift in the cultural crises of the times and often turned to cults, cranks, or gurus who offered security and certain answers. The craving for instant and certain salvation was not limited to college campuses or to the under-thirty generation, but it was primarily a youth movement. Margaret Singer, professor of psychiatry at the University of California at San Francisco, stresses, however, one critical difference between the cultists now and those of the past. Cults traditionally sought out the socially marginal. More recently they have attracted mainly white, middle-class college students or recent graduates who are looking for abstract, philosophical principles to add to an already economically secure life. These people live in what seems to them a spiritually, morally, and emotionally bland world, but they have a desire to be caring and altruistic and to do something good for humankind. Basically, they are seeking a secure guide to meaning in life, and they have not found it in mainline churches or other institutions. "The ironic fact," says Dr. Singer, "is that before the upheaval of the sixties most of these people would have found what they were now looking for in the traditional life of the family and in the public service."[32] Now their idealism can lead them directly to a cult.

According to Houston psychiatrist Harvey A. Rosenstock, cults often have flourished with revolution—the French Revolution or the Industrial Revolution, for example. They have always thrived during a period of rapid social change and pressure. When there is a change in the basic matrix of society, and the traditional seats of authority shift, then people are cut loose from their bases of security and are especially open to attraction to a cult. Our country is still caught up in a radical cultural and philosophical revolution which originated in the 1960s. Many look for, and apparently find, relief from today's social and moral crises in cultism. Currently there is a feeling of uncertainty among the young; often they are the in-betweens—in between love affairs, moving from high school to college, from one job to another, facing identity issues, dealing with alienation—and they are prime targets for cultic missionaries.[33]

As a person is recruited gently, subtly, and lovingly into a cult, he typically is isolated physically and socially from mainstream society.

In return, the cult provides a world-view—a sweeping philosophy explaining everything, answering all questions, clearing all confusion, and relieving frustration. The cult thus provides a source of authority, a foundation of belief, and a ready, supportive peer group. Any questions are sent up the chain of command, and answers come back from the final higher authority. It is a perfect way of life for people who require instant answers. The cult appears to provide a smooth path and promises ideals difficult to disagree with: brotherhood, equality, the good life, an end to anxiety, relaxation, supporting peers, and instant experience.

The "smooth path" usually leads to an inward turning for individual experience in a quest for self-discovery, and a backing away from social doctrines. The cult's system offers salvation on faith alone—a radical faith in its system. This process is a dangerous retreat from knowledge and reason, back into mysticism and emotionalism, both of which have a place in a complete system of religion.

The Unification Church (Moonies), founded by Sun Myung Moon, a Korean clergyman, while radically different from the "Jesus people," the Children of God, or the flower children, is representative, if not typical, of the cultist trend. In their mode of operation, the Moonies invite an "uncertain youth" to dinner and a discussion of moral issues. This sounds worthy and normal enough. The visitor basks in the extravagant compliments and the warm personal support that are extended. Then follows a weekend of fellowship and discussion, and then longer periods of time together at relatively remote places. Fellowship is provided; a need to tie one's life firmly to some meaningful group task is established. A tight system of beliefs is presented, which easily displaces the slim residue of faith picked up from occasional Sunday school attendance in an orthodox church. Surprisingly, the lectures at Unification centers are long, complicated, and heavy, and yet young people seem willing to sit through them and work to understand them. Presently the visitor is conditioned right into the group, and until he is a true believer his experiences are monitored and guided to guarantee group loyalty. The previously uncertain youth now has supportive friends, a tight belief-system answering all questions, and a program of activities geared to bring the Moonie messianic hope. Now the novitiate who was cut loose in a valueless society has a world-view for which to live and work! Most other cults, while radically different in broad objectives, fulfill these same basic life-orientation needs.

The need for meaning and relationships in life could be fully met by the orthodox church if it would fulfill its fellowship, worship, and outreach missions; then there would be no need for the cult. However, all too often the average Christian church seems to be bland and ineffectual. Even young people from churchgoing families often have a poor image of the church. On the other hand, spirited, evangelical, conservative churches often appear to be strong and effective. Generally these groups are growing, and there is a clear parallel between their appeal and that of the cult.

The traditional Christian minister might like to call down fire on all cults, when the necessity is to seek what they have that is so attractive. The preacher may well find a truth to use in his or her own preaching ministry, or may discover the omission of some basic thrust that speaks to very real needs—particularly those of young people in this day of the new morality.

NON-CHURCH FACTORS

We have been discussing those occurrences of the twentieth century that have had particular ecclesiastical application. The list is not meant to be definitive; it includes only those "news" items of interest to the church. The routine matters of evangelism, Christian education, new church development, missions, and the like, have continued to receive due consideration.

But apart from the obviously church-related events and trends, many other things have been developing in the last eighty years, and they must have the attention of any preacher who expects to communicate the gospel in the framework of contemporary thought and culture. These other things are the preoccupations of society—the ideas and events in which people are caught up—the concerns a preacher must know about in order to present the message of the kingdom of God in the idiom of "now." This was the way of Jesus as he likened the kingdom of heaven to the "now" of his day—the sower, the steward, the prodigal son, and the robbers on their way to Jericho.

The experts who study trends and causative factors in society have had a lot to say about changes in American life in this century, particularly in the last three decades. Without much difficulty, we can find explanations and justifications for almost everything our society has done and is doing; some changes are obvious, some are subtle, some are insidious. For instance, no one would argue that we (and the rest of the world) have made incredible scientific and technological progress—the laser, bioengineering, health science, automation, the space program. We have progressed sociologically—women, youth, minorities, and older people are finding places, jobs, and acceptance; cities are being reclaimed and restored; we have more leisure—even a four-day workweek, in some places. Politically, we have not done so well. We as a nation have lost face and prestige, for various reasons. We live in an uneasy truce with third-world nations. We live with the threat of nuclear war.

These are the obvious concerns but there have been and will continue to be subtle and insidious repercussions—dwindling energy sources, man/machine competition, widespread use of mind-altering drugs, boredom, the credit-card economy, faltering educational systems, the loss of single-family dwellings and the increase in the number of transient apartment people, the diminishing integrity of the family, youth/age disparity. On the latter issue, Margaret Mead had a point.

> The culture in which the young [now] live is so different that the old can give them little guidance in how to deal with it. The young take for granted satellites, war, computers, pollution, the idea of population control. . . . The older generation is similarly isolated and knows more about change than any other generation. . . . The young must be allowed to participate directly and ask questions; however, there must exist enough trust between generations so that the old will be allowed to work on the answers.[34]

Our society in this century has become increasingly more sensate and hedonistic. We are involved in a continuing quest for freedom; yet we want stability, assurance, authority, and love. We want all that technology has to offer; but we want our open fields, clean water, and air. We want everything!

The fast moving and exciting features of twentieth-century existence, which are made universally known almost instantly through the media, grip the lives of people. The informed preacher who is aware of these things is able not only to share the gospel message framed in early Middle Eastern language and imagery, but can set it in the context of "now." That preacher can preach to people where they are; and only there can they be reached.

V. PREACHING:
PRINCIPLES AND PROMISE

Two tasks remain: (1) to articulate some principles that have become evident as we have sketched the tradition of preaching; and (2) to make some predictions about the promise of preaching—its future in an uncertain world.

PRINCIPLES OF PREACHING

So vast a body of literature as all the sermons preached during the past two thousand years makes generalizing a hazardous occupation. Further complicating that task is the variety of political and theological settings in which that preaching has been done. Some principles seem to emerge, however, and they may provide some focus for this final chapter, which attempts, in part, to define the preaching tradition.

The progressive church preaches.

Preaching has not always been central in the work of the Christian church, contrary to what we might like to believe. There have been times when the practice of preaching was almost nonexistent—notably, but not only, in the Middle Ages. There have been times when, sadly, liturgy and sacraments became the focal point of worship, to the detriment of preaching. On occasion, the clergy have not been well enough prepared to be willing or able to preach. And there have been times when the church has wielded such political power and has been so satisfied with its position that it felt little need to preach.

But when the church has been alive, vibrant, sharing, and expanding, then preaching has been central; at times when the church has been corrupt, preaching has been used as an instrument of reform; in missionary expansion, preaching has been a central tool. The progressive church preaches.

Preaching is revelation.

While preaching has not always been central in the practice of the church, its very nature identifies it with the central function of the church, which is to bring God and people together. Certainly Jesus commanded the church to preach. The successful example of apostolic preaching encourages the church to preach. Preaching builds and solidifies the understanding and faith of the church; the church is extended as the gospel is proclaimed. But the very nature of preaching makes it central. *God speaks through preaching. Preaching is revelation.* The most significant preaching has grown out of a Word-of-God theology of preaching; it is preaching that communicates God's Word to humankind, through human speech.

Preaching at its best, then, is sacramental; it is that point of communion between the responding person and the presence of God; it is a genuine avenue of grace. This is not to say that the sacramental function is always performed in preaching, for either the preacher or the listener may not perform aright. And spellbinding eloquence in the pulpit is not necessarily preaching in the sacramental sense, if the substance of the preaching is not clearly a part of the kerygma or the didache. The tradition of the church well may be the substance of sermons, but such usage must be measured by compatibility with the biblical witness to the Word. On the other hand, even with simple, clear, compelling gospel, all or part of a given congregation may be so preoccupied with ideas other than the Word that they cannot give affirming response. But preaching at its best is the Word of God experienced by both preacher and listener.

Kerygma and *didache* speak to different persons.

The distinction between *kerygma* and *didache* in both content and practice is important. The New Testament and the Church Fathers clearly indicated that the purpose of the preaching of the kerygma was to extend the church, and it was consequently proclaimed to the unchurched world. On the other hand, didache involved sharing the teachings of Jesus and interpreting the kerygma to Christians—helping them to understand and apply what they heard. The church now, as then, must understand for itself and pass on to the next generation the teaching of the Lord (didache), but it is by kerygma that "it has pleased God to save men." The unevangelized need something other than didache; the evangelized need more than kerygma. Certainly God honors each of these types of preaching.

Preaching aims at specific targets.

Sermons are not preached *in general*, but for particular people with particular needs in particular places. Preparation for preaching must include not only basic homiletic skills, but a knowledge of and a concern for the elements in society that affect the listeners. Abuse of this responsibility has been a perennial barrier to sharing the Word, throughout the history of the Christian church. In a parish setting the minister learns to know and comes to care for his or her people and consequently is aware of their desires and their needs. The pastor thus is well equipped to interpret the gospel to the congregation.

Preaching and liturgy complement each other.

We often speak of the ministries of Word and Sacrament as if they were two different aspects of ministry. They both serve the same essential purpose: that God may reveal himself to us. For those who have been initiated into the meaning of the faith, the liturgy and the sacraments speak eloquently and meaningfully so that within them the Word may again become alive. This realization of the presence of God is based on recalled experience. It is efficient and effective in conserving and solidifying ideas and values to which one already has given assent. As evangelical preaching most often has come *before* liturgy, so it also goes *beyond*—to instruct, and to provide opportunity for growth and maturation, and to move hearers to new commitments.

Some churches have placed heavy emphasis on liturgy, to the essential exclusion of preaching; on the other hand, some of the freer Protestant churches have so emphasized preaching that they have not made efficient use of liturgies, which could assume an effective place in their services. The latter approach places an extremely heavy responsibility on the preacher to generate new ideas, new experiences, new revelations, and a new presence of the Word at each preaching service.

It is idle to place sacraments in opposition to preaching—both serve a common, communicative, conserving-of-the-faith function—and the basic question in a given circumstance should be, What use of Word or Sacrament will honor God at this moment?

Preaching requires called, competent persons.

Our survey has suggested that all kinds of people may be useful as Christian ministers, but that true regeneration, a distinct awareness of a call from God, and a God-serving motivation are requisites for a preaching ministry. Christians have often differed on the nature of conversion, but all have agreed on the necessity for a truly regenerated ministry. The call to preach may come as a personal one, or it may come to a congregation or to a judicatory, as a directive to set someone apart. However it comes, the effective minister must be profoundly aware of the summons from God. The preacher is not simply a reporter, but a witness to the kerygma: Voice, face, total aura—all testify that "I have been caught up in this thing."

Style, composition, length, literary content, and delivery style all are concerns of the individual preacher, and great preaching has come from vastly dissimilar people, places, behaviors, and even theologies. But the people who have done it best have been those who have had a lofty view of the nature of preaching and have taken their task seriously.

Apart from these things, an effective minister should be a person of integrity; willing to learn; competent in scripture, theology, church polity, and an understanding of the sacraments; and as we have emphasized, must be aware of the current culture—those ideas, movements, and other things in which people are caught up. Most preachers are no longer the "persons" of the community; many congregants who face a preacher on Sunday have equally strong or better academic backgrounds. But the person in the pulpit must never permit the office to be embarrassed, as has happened on occasion, by failure to study, to prepare, and to be a holy instrument of God, searching out answers to the ultimate questions of the sacred and speaking to the people for God. To again quote Humbert de Romans, "It is very difficult to reach perfection in preaching."

Emphasizing preaching unifies the ministry.

The typical Christian minister is called upon to be many things: counselor, educator, pastor, administrator, custodian, carpenter, preacher. It is sometimes difficult to insist that the primary responsibility is that of preaching, or interpreting the Word. This has been the distinctive, necessary task of the minister in every age; nothing else is as important; nothing can substitute for it. Lay people can be and increasingly will be trained for many of the other tasks. Placing the preaching task first will allow the minister to organize other responsibilities around it and will unify the work, giving coherence and balance to other jobs. The more a minister works at preaching, the more he or she will

> discover a sense of orderliness in his ministries of paperclips and memoranda, telephone calls and afternoon teas; the more he will know who he is and what his game is and what the rules of the game are. He will gradually cease to think of himself as a religious cowboy wearing a red, white, and blue "I like God" button on his chest and trying to keep his feet in the stirrups of a bucking, jolting, piece of ecclesiastical machinery that nobody to his knowledge has stayed on very long.[1]

Preaching changes people.

The preaching of vital Christian truths, with any measure of adaptation to human needs, finds people ready to listen. Unhappily, many preach without the life and warmth or the attention to contemporary interests and needs that are so necesssary to make the gospel attractive and contagious. On the other hand, some become so involved in preaching about timely political, social, and cultural matters that they overlook the basic ideas and ideals of the gospel. The preacher who can present the Lord's message, applying it to the trials, frustrations, sins, sufferings, and joys of our present society, will surely be instrumental in bringing the listeners to the central meaning of life and in leaving them in the presence of God.

The church cannot fail to preach.

Preaching of the kerygma is inherent in the nature of the church. Jesus commanded his church to preach the gospel, but beyond that, the church, as a redeemed fellowship, is urged by an inner prompting to share its most prized possession: the gospel message contained in the basic kerygmatic New Testament message. Certainly the gospel can be understood by means other than preaching, and certainly God speaks in other ways than through the sermon, but preaching occupies and will continue to occupy a primary place in the worship and life of a church that wishes to be dynamic and useful. It moves the people by presenting a godly vision of where the church ought to be.

The Christian church will continue to prosper because of the ministers God sends to it, for the ministry as an institution is God's gift to his church. The minister, as a servant of the Word, is an apostle to the church. As a vehicle of the gospel, the church provides an opportunity for the fulfillment of the basic human search for meaning in life. Preaching is basically a summons to a discovery of that meaning. Where the Word is preached clearly, simply, and compellingly to people in their current situations, there God works among his people. Such preaching brings the people to Christ by bringing Christ to the people, and therein lies the greatness, the challenge, and the joy of the calling of the preacher.

THE PROMISE OF PREACHING

The future is not set, and surely that, too, is a gift of God. But there is in all history, including that of the church, a basic continuum of thought and action that may suggest the events of tomorrow. What is the future for preaching?

Ministry and preaching will continue.

Religion deals with ultimate questions and answers and requires time-consuming study and analysis. Most of us are unwilling to do this for ourselves, so we need a religious servant—a minister—to study and report findings on the basic questions of life. A major new theory concerning the origin of psychiatric disorders points to our basic frustration in finding meaning in life. We have a profound longing for meaning, yet we want to keep the sacred at arm's length. The ministry, then, functions to fill an ongoing, almost universal need to understand the sacred. Perhaps the day will come when people will have the free time to do their own questing. If this happens the parish ministry may be less necessary, but the need for theologians would remain, so that they might guide the searchers.

But the prediction is that not just the ministry, but preaching, will continue. Preaching is an efficient and effective performance of ministry. How else can so many, so quickly and so effectively, participate not only in an experience of the sacred but in the warmth of redeeming Christian fellowship? Jesus commanded us to preach, and preaching will continue because people, both in and out of the church, knowing its influence for good, do not want it to stop.

Ritual will survive and prosper.

Ritual is a part of humanity's quest for the sacred. It is a quick and efficient way to recall profound religious experiences for reaffirmation and new commitment. It is a stereotyped, concentrated set of symbols, expressing beliefs and sentiments regarding ultimate things.

Ritual will not only survive, but it will change and prosper with modern sophisticated media, to meet the needs and expectations of our better-educated society. As long as we have preaching of the kerygma, we will have ritual to conserve and to express the results of proclamation.

The number of women in ministry will increase markedly.

Concurrent with the freedom movements of the 1960s, the women's liberation movement has had a widely accepted impact on our society. Growing out of that thrust came the ordination of eleven women into the priesthood in the Church of the Advocate in Philadelphia on July 29, 1974. This marked the fall of the last major barrier to women clergy in American Protestantism. Now women comprise some 25 percent of the enrollment in major Protestant seminaries and larger numbers are becoming eligible for the ministry of Word and Sacrament.

Roman Catholic and Eastern Orthodox Christians still hold firmly to their practice of an all-male clergy, although the issue in Roman Catholicism is a matter of discipline, rather than doctrine, and thus may change as times and needs of the church change. Resistance to the ordination of women is being undermined by the growing shortage of priests and the decreasing number of seminarians. Women have been very successful in places of leadership in the Roman Catholic church—in religious orders, in schools, in universities, and in hospitals. Further, with hierarchical concession that the deaconesses of the early church were actually in sacred orders, and given the urgency and pervasiveness of the feminist movement, it is quite likely that women will have the opportunity for full ordination in all Christian groups in the foreseeable future.

And with ordination, of course, comes the office of preaching. Since women have proven their academic capabilities in clerical studies and have been excellent speakers in many areas, we have every reason to believe, even with little precedent, that they will be fine preachers and that the field of preaching will be strengthened by their presence.

The laity will play a larger role in the church, and this will affect preaching.

The expanding role of the laity in the church grows from a radical reassessment of the nature of the church, associated with the human rights revolution of the 1960s. Lay persons, many with better educational backgrounds and more leisure time than the clergy, will have more opportunity for participation in the pastoral and teaching functions of the church. Also, with increased freedom from the requirements of labor in our technological society, people will seek answers to ultimate questions. Undoubtedly, they will discover that secular pursuits will not provide those answers, and they will turn more and more to the church to find supportive bases for life. This turning to the church will be further supported by the accessibility of the neighborhood congregation, in a time of growing immobility of society due to the energy crunch. Laity's increased participation in the church and in the duties normally performed by the clergy will free the minister's time and energy for devotion to preaching.

Protestant parochial schools may increase, with a resulting influence on preaching.

The establishment of parochial schools has been a regular practice of Catholics and Quakers, a frequent practice of Seventh-day Adventists, an occasional practice of Lutherans, and a rare policy for Baptists, Methodists, and Presbyterians. Generally such schools have been founded to provide an understanding of the basics of the faith, in the face of threats. Catholics established parochial schools in the United States because public schools were essentially Protestant until the middle of our century. Now public schools, as a result of Supreme Court rulings and strong secular humanist teachers, are barely religious and certainly not Protestant. It is now unthinkable that the public schools would grant academic credit for Sunday school attendance, as was once a standard practice.

The often junglelike conditions and declining academic achievement in our schools is provoking widespread disillusionment and dissatisfaction with public education and urging some alternative. The church is probably the only viable institution able to provide that alternative. It seems increasingly true that more and more mainline Christians, not to mention militant conservatives, are willing to pay what is necessary for the stable moral influence and Christian education of parochial schools.

The system of parochial education lays the foundation for initiation into the faith and, in essence, becomes the preacher. The laity then may provide communicant and confirmation exercises, freeing the minister for pastoral and prophetic preaching in a church and society considerably stabilized by parochial education. This will be a matter of concern for preachers of the next generation, since it could revolutionize the Christian-education mission of the church, as well as its relationship to public institutions.

Preaching will improve in quality and quantity.

American preaching will be more widespread, and it will be of better quality.[2] This may be attributed to several factors: markedly better teaching of preaching in the seminaries; widespread and vastly improved continuing-education programs for our preachers; and the common idiom of our country, which grows out of an almost universal viewing of television.

But these factors merely occasion the growing use of preaching. The root cause of this trend is the changed nature of society, marked by a higher educational level and more free time, which has resulted in a wider seeking of ultimate answers for an acceptable philosophy of life. In this seeking, liturgy will continue to have its place within the church, but the new, educated, freed-from-drudgry, meaning-seeking person wants to go beyond the experiences of liturgy that merely recall and renew old commitments. This "new person" seeks answers beyond liturgical experiences. Preaching is the means through which the church can provide answers for the questions of modern people and can supply experiences in the meaning of the gospel applied in contemporary society.

Today's people, in their quest for understanding of the gospel, now will accept no less than thorough and exciting preaching, speaking to all of life. They are increasingly of the mind and temperament of one British monarch, who is reported to have demanded of a clergyman fulminating before him, "Either talk sense or come down."[3] The expectation of excellence in preaching by more and more lay people will turn more resources to schools and seminaries. The new seminary graduate can be so prepared that he or she goes to the first pastorate, not just as a well-trained scholar, but as an effective and stimulating preacher as well.

NOTES

CHAPTER I—Preaching: The Early Heritage

1. John A. Broadus, *Lectures on the History of Preaching* (New York: Armstrong, 1902), pp. 1-12.
2. G. Ernest Wright, *The Old Testament Against Its Environment: Studies in Biblical Theology* (Chicago: Henry Regnery Co., 1950), p. 116.
3. *Encyclopedia Judaica*, 1971 ed., 13:994.
4. Kenneth Scott Latourette, *A History of Christianity* (New York: Harper & Brothers, 1953), pp. 36-37.
5. Broadus, *Lectures*, p. 235.
6. Latourette, *History of Christianity*, *p. 65*.
7. *Charles H. Dodd, The Apostolic Preaching and Its Developments: Three Lectures With an Appendix on Eschatology and History* (New York: Harper & Row, 1964), p. 27.
8. Claude H. Thompson, *Theology of the Kerygma* (Englewood Cliffs, N.J.: Prentice-Hall, 1962), pp. 3-4.
9. *The Great Sermons of the Great Preachers, Ancient and Modern: With an Historical Sketch of the Greek and Latin Pulpit* (London: Ward and Lock, 1858), p. 2.
10. *Ibid.*, pp. 5-6.
11. *Ibid.*, p. 8.
12. Thomas Merton, *Basic Principles of Monastic Spirituality* (Gethsemani, Ky.: Abbey of Gethsemani; 1957), p. 3.
13. John M'Clintock and James Strong, *Cyclopedia of Biblical, Theological, and Ecclesiastical Literature*, 12 vols. (New York: Harper & Brothers, 1879), 8:482.
14. Andrew M. Greeley, *The Crucible of Change: The Social Dynamics of Pastoral Practice* (New York: Sheed & Ward, 1968), p. 104.
15. H. G. Wells, *The Outline of History*, 2 vols. (Garden City, N.Y.: Doubleday & Co., 1961), 1:439.

CHAPTER II—Preaching: Decline and Renewal

1. William Habberton and Lawrence V. Roth, *Man's Achievements Through the Ages* (Atlanta: Laidlaw Brothers, 1956), p. 164.

2. *Encyclopedia of Southern Baptists*, 2 vols. (Nashville: Broadman Press, 1958), 2:1104.

3. Yngve T. Brilioth, *Landmarks in the History of Preaching* (London: S.P.C.K., 1950), p. 13.

4. John A. Broadus, *Lectures on the History of Preaching* (New York: Armstrong, 1902), p. 109.

5. Brilioth, *Landmarks*, p. 13.

6. *Ibid.*, p. 17.

7. John Brown, *Puritan Preaching in England* (New York: Charles Scribner's Sons, 1900), p. 18.

8. T. C. O'Brien, ed., *Corpus Dictionary of Western Churches* (Washington, D.C.: Corpus Publications, 1970), p. 609.

9. Winthrop S. Hudson, *Religion in America* (New York: Charles Scribner's Sons, 1973), p. 57.

10. H. A. Oberman, "Preaching and the Word in the Reformation," *Theology Today*, April 1961, p. 17.

11. John Killinger, *The Centrality of Preaching in the Total Task of the Ministry* (Waco, Tex.: Word Books, 1969), p. 44.

12. Hudson, *Religion in America*, pp. 66-67.

CHAPTER III—Preaching: America—to 1900

1. William Warren Sweet, *Religion in Colonial America* (New York: Charles Scribner's Sons, 1942), p. 117.

2. Arthur Stephen Hoyt, *The Pulpit and American Life* (New York: The Macmillan Co., 1921), p. 9.

3. *Ibid.*, p. 12.

4. Sweet, *Religion*, p. 278.

5. Winthrop S. Hudson, *Religion in America* (New York: Charles Scribner's Sons, 1973), p. 96.

6. Robert V. Friedenberg, " 'With a Firm Reliance on the Protection of Divine Providence': Colonial Pulpit Rhetoric and the Coming of the Revolution" (Paper presented at the Speech Communication Association national convention, Houston, Texas, December 1975).

7. Statistics from Sweet, *Religion*, pp. 37-38.

8. Sydney E. Ahlstrom, *A Religious History of the United States* (New Haven: Yale University Press, 1972), p. 433.

9. *Ibid.*, p. 748.

CHAPTER IV—Preaching: Twentieth-Century America

1. William Warren Sweet, *The Story of Religion in America* (New York: Harper & Brothers, 1950), pp. 391-92.

2. John T. Stewart, *The Deacon Wore Spats: Profiles from America's Changing Religious Scene* (New York: Holt, Rinehart, & Winston, 1965), p. 47.

3. *Ibid.*, p. 57.

4. Robert T. Handy, *The American Religious Depression 1925–1935* (Philadelphia: Fortress Press, 1968), p. 5. This study was originally published in *Church History*, 29 (1960): 3-16.

5. DeWitte T. Holland, ed., *Sermons in American History* (Nashville: Abingdon Press, 1969), pp. 404 ff.
6. *NCCC Chronicle*, Summer 1978.
7. Clyde Reid, *21st Century Man: Emerging* (Philadelphia: United Church Press, 1971), p. 75.
8. Jackson W. Carroll, "Church in the World," *Theology Today*, April 1978, p. 70.
9. Patrick McNamara, ed., *Religion American Style* (New York: Harper & Row, 1974), p. 296.
10. Sydney E. Ahlstrom, *A Religious History of the United States* (New Haven: Yale University Press, 1972), p. 1074.
11. Winthrop S. Hudson, *Religion in America* (New York: Charles Scribner's Sons, 1973), p. 435.
12. Handy, *American Religious Depression*, p. 20.
13. John Tracy Ellis, "American Catholicism 1953–1979: A Notable Change," *Thought: A Review of Culture and Idea*, June 1979, p. 117.
14. Hudson, *Religion in America*, p. 395.
15. *Ibid.*, p. 407.
16. *The Program of Priestly Formation of the National Conference of Catholic Bishops, United States of America*, 2d ed. (Washington, D.C.: Publications Office, National Conference of Catholic Bishops, 1976), p. 37.
17. Jean-Francois Ravel, *Without Marx or Jesus* (Garden City, N.Y.: Doubleday & Co., 1971), p. 200.
18. Ahlstrom, *Religious History*, p. 1087.
19. "Shall Women Speak?" *Journal of Presbyterian History*, Winter 1978, p. 281.
20. "Women Priests," *The Witness*, June 1978.
21. *Time*, 22 October 1979, p. 67.
22. Elsie Gibson, "Ecumenism and the Ordination of Women," *Crosscurrents*, Fall 1978, p. 303.
23. Charles E. Swann, "The Electric Church," *Presbyterian Survey*, May 1979.
24. *Ibid.*
25. William Martin, "Heavenly Hosts," *Texas Monthly*, March 1979, pp. 124-25.
26. *Ibid.*, p. 129.
27. William F. Fore, "The Electric Church," *Ministry*, January 1979, p. 6.
28. James S. Tinney, "William J. Seymour, Father of Modern Day Pentecostalism," *Journal of the Interdenominational Theological Center*, Fall 1977, p. 34.
29. Martin E. Marty, *A Nation of Behavers* (Chicago: University of Chicago Press, 1976), p. 123.
30. John F. McArthur, Jr., *The Charismatics: A Doctrinal Perspective* (Grand Rapids: Zondervan Publishing House, 1978), p. 224.
31. Hudson, *Religion in America*, p. 431.
32. C. Fuller, "Cults on Campus," *Ladies Home Journal*, May 1979, p. 42.
33. *Houston Chronicle*, 11 February 1979.
34. Cited by David Wallechinsky and Irving Wallace, *The People's Almanac* (Garden City, N.Y.: Doubleday & Co., 1975), p. 25.

CHAPTER V—Preaching: Principles and Promise

1. John Killinger, *The Centrality of Preaching in the Total Task of the Ministry* (Waco, Tex.: Word Books, 1969), pp. 26-27.
2. See "American Preaching: A Dying Art?" *Time*, 31 December 1979.
3. Killinger, *Centrality of Preaching*, p. 3.

FOR FURTHER READING

The numbers in parentheses following each entry refer to the chapters to which the works are most relevant.

Ahlstrom, Sydney E. *A Religious History of the United States*. New Haven: Yale University Press, 1972. (3, 4)

Barth, Karl. *The Preaching of the Gospel*. Philadelphia: Westminster Press, 1963. (Intro., 5)

Berger, Peter L. *The Noise of Solemn Assemblies: Christian Commitment and the Religious Establishment in America*. Garden City, N. Y.: Doubleday & Co., 1961. (4)

Brilioth, Yngve. *A Brief History of Preaching*. Philadelphia: Fortress Press, 1965. (1, 2)

————. *Landmarks in the History of Preaching*. London: S.P.C.K., 1950. (1, 2)

Broadus, John A. *Lectures on the History of Preaching*. New York: Armstrong, 1902. (1, 2, 3)

Brown, John. *Puritan Preaching in England*. New York: Charles Scribner's Sons, 1900. (2)

Dargan, Edwin C. *A History of Preaching*. London: Hodder & Stoughton, 1905. (1, 2, 3)

Dodd, Charles. *The Apostolic Preaching and Its Developments: Three Lectures with an Appendix on Eschatology and History*. New York: Harper & Row, 1964 (1)

The Great Sermons of the Great Preachers, Ancient and Modern: With an Historical Sketch of the Greek and Latin Pulpit. London: Ward and Lock, 1858. (1, 2)

Greeley, Andrew M. *The American Catholic: A Social Portrait*. New York: Basic Books, 1977. (3, 4)

————. *The Catholic Experience: An Interpretation of the History of American Catholicism*. New York: Doubleday & Co., 1967. (3, 4)

Gustafson, James M., ed. *The Sixties: Radical Change in American Religion*. Philadelphia: American Academy of Political and Social Science, 1970. (4)

Handy, Robert T. *The Social Gospel in America, 1870–1920*. New York: Oxford University Press, 1966. (4)

Holland, DeWitte T., ed. *Preaching in American History*. Nashville: Abingdon Press, 1969. (3, 4)

Howe, R. L. "Overcoming Barriers to Communication." *Princeton Seminary Bulletin*, May 1963, pp. 44-52. (4, 5)

————. "Recovery of Dialogue in Preaching." *Pastoral Psychology*, October 1961, pp. 10-14. (5)

Hudson, Winthrop S. *Religion in America*. New York: Charles Scribner's Sons, 1973. (3, 4)

Ker, John. *Lectures on the History of Preaching*. London: Hodder and Stoughton, 1889. (1, 2)

Kerr, Hugh Thomas. *Preaching in the Early Church*. New York: Fleming H. Revell, 1942. (1)

Killinger, John. *The Centrality of Preaching in the Total Task of the Ministry*. Waco, Tex.: Word Books, 1969. (4, 5)

Marty, Martin E. *A Nation of Behavers*. Chicago: The University of Chicago Press, 1976. (4)

Mitchell, Henry E. *Black Preaching*. Philadelphia: J. B. Lippincott, 1970. (3, 4)

Nelson, John Wiley. *Your God Is Alive and Well and Appearing in Popular Culture*. Philadelphia: Westminster Press, 1976. (4)

Oberman, H. A. "Preaching and the Word in the Reformation." *Harvard Divinity Bulletin*, October 1960, pp. 7-18. (2)

Pike, James A. *A New Look in Preaching*. New York: Charles Scribner's Sons, 1961. (4, 5)

Raboteau, Albert J. *Slave Religion: The "Invisible Institution" in the Antebellum South*. New York: Oxford University Press, 1978. (3)

Reid, Clyde H. *The Empty Pulpit*. New York: Harper & Brothers, 1947. (4, 5)

————. *21st Century Man—Emerging*. Philadelphia: United Church Press, 1971. (4, 5)

Shelton, Robert M. "Preaching—Now!" *Austin Seminary Bulletin*, September 1972, pp. 1-32. (4, 5)

INDEX

251.00973
N 73